Writing: Steps to Success
Level 3 to 4 +

Kevin Eames Karyn Taylor David Trelawny-Ross
Consultant: Debra Myhill

Hodder & Stoughton

A MEMBER OF THE HODDER HEADLINE GROUP

Acknowledgements

The publishers would like to thank the following for their kind permission to reproduce copyright material:

Copyright Text:

ppix–x two extracts from English Text Mark Scheme, 2000 © Qualifications and Curriculum Authority; pp8, 11, 14, 16, all extracts from *Tom Fobble's Day* by Alan Garner © Alan Garner. Reproduced by permission of the author and David Higham Associates; p27 The Severn Bore Page © Russell Higgins 2001. Reproduced by kind permission of the author; p30 'Going Down Gorgeous' from *Getaway Adventure Guide* by Jennifer Stern © Jennifer Stern; p50 AOL advertisement © 2001 AOL (UK) Ltd. Used with permission; p54 'Lets go full throttle to catch roadhogs', a letter which appeared in *The Mirror*, August 14, 2001 © *The Mirror*; p54 'Why are we served last?' from Your Shout which appeared in *The Newspaper*, Issue 3 September 2000 © *The Newspaper*; p58 'I Can't Talk to Boys!', an extract from *Shout Magazine* © DC Thomson & Co., Ltd. Reproduced by kind permission of DC Thomson & Co., Ltd.; p71 a restaurant review of Brook's Restaurant by Diane Broughton, which appeared in *The Big Issue in the North*. Reproduced by kind permission of the author and *The Big Issue in the North*.

Copyright Photographs:

p28 a photograph of tidal bore surfers on the Severn Bore © Bristol Evening Post; p36 Victoria Falls, Zimbabwe © Nik Wheeler/Corbis; p36 Rapids on Kings River © Marc Muench/Corbis; p58 Boy and Girl Talking at Wall © Richard Hutchings/Corbis; p67 male tennis player © Corel.

Copyright Artworks:

Pat Murray: pp 1, 3, 14–15, 18, 21, 24, 29, 31, 33, 38–39, 45, 52, 56, 60, 65, 68, 73, 77.
Doug Gray: pp 8, 12–13, 16, 28, 54.
David Hancock: pp 2, 23, 46, 67.

Every effort has been made to trace copyright holders of material reproduced in this book. Any notice not acknowledged will be acknowledged in subsequent printings if notice is given to the publisher.

Orders: please contact Bookpoint Ltd, 130 Milton Park, Abingdon, Oxon OX14 4SB. Telephone: (44) 01235 827720, Fax: (44) 01235 400454. Lines are open from 9.00 – 6.00, Monday to Saturday, with a 24 hour message answering service. You can also order through our website www.hodderheadline.co.uk

British Library Cataloguing in Publication Data
A catalogue record for this title is available from The British Library

ISBN 0 340 84518 X

First published 2002
Impression number   10 9 8 7 6 5 4 3 2
Year   2008 2007 2006 2005 2004 2003

Copyright © 2002 Kevin Eames, Karyn Taylor, David Trelawny-Ross

Cover photo from Michael Stones
Typeset by Fakenham Photosetting Limited, Fakenham, Norfolk
Printed in Great Britain for Hodder & Stoughton Educational, a division of Hodder Headline, 338 Euston Road, London NW1 3BH by J.W. Arrowsmiths, Bristol.

CONTENTS

Teachers' Introduction

This book:

1   places continual emphasis on letting students know exactly what they need to do for success at a particular level

2   breaks down success into bite-size achievable targets, particularly relevant to the learning needs of boys

3   covers all the different text-types in the Key Stage 3 Literacy Framework

4   focuses on sentence level work, to improve students' control over sentence construction

5   draws on approaches to writing embodied in the Key Stage 3 Literacy Strategy and the Progress Units

6   is designed to be used either with specific ability groups, in a mixed ability class, or with different year groups

7   aims to keep the writing process real.

This book:

1   places continual emphasis on letting students know exactly what they need to do for success at a particular level

Writing: Steps to Success is intended to help students who are currently working at a specified level to improve their writing skills so that they are able, independently, to write at a higher level. It aims to do this by giving students a detailed awareness of what writing at their target level looks like, and by making sure they are clear about what exactly they need to do to write at that level. Each book begins with a detailed comparison of two pieces of writing by students, one at the lower and the other at the upper level. Accompanying the texts is a thorough commentary, making very explicit the distinct features that differentiate the two texts from each other. The aim is to help students to be very clear about the skills they need to develop to progress from the lower to the upper level, or to consolidate and broaden their achievement if they are already beginning to write at the upper level.

2 breaks down success into bite-size achievable targets, particularly relevant to the learning needs of boys

Each book breaks down the skills needed to write at each level into a set of small achievable targets. As is now generally recognised, boys in particular benefit from having it made very clear to them what exactly they need to do, in small steps, to make progress. Each unit, therefore, breaks down the task of writing a particular text-type into the separate skills, mastery of which is needed to write at the level the student is working towards. In addition, each book builds on the skills learnt in the previous book. There is, therefore, a clear progression in the skills being taught so that students grow in confidence and complexity with which they are able to demonstrate the skills essential for successful writing. Each book also focuses on the objectives of one year: **Writing: Steps to Success Level 3 to 4**⁺ uses the Framework Objectives for Year 7 as a starting point. Together, therefore, the three books provide a chronological progression as well as a skills progression.

3 covers all the different text-types in the Key Stage 3 Literacy Framework

In organisation, **Writing: Steps to Success** is very simple and clear. At the beginning of each book is a Students' Introduction with examples of students' work at the lower and upper levels relevant to that book. Through a discussion of these, students are able to form a clear picture of the differences in writing at the two levels, and to begin establishing their own targets for the skills they need to improve their own writing. Each book then has four units, each unit guiding students through the production of a piece of writing in each of the text-type triplets described in the Key Stage 3 Literacy Framework and National Curriculum 2000 document. In doing this, it ensures that the main text and sentence level objectives in the Literacy Framework for Key Stage 3 Writing are covered.

4 focuses on sentence level work, to improve students' control over sentence construction

The books do not aim to cover all the text and sentence level objectives. However, there is a continual emphasis on improving students' ability to control and extend their sentences, this being essential to success at a higher level. As a result, within each unit, there is a significant emphasis on developing their sentence level skills and all the sentence level objectives that are important in moving students from one level to the next are covered.

5   draws on approaches to writing embodied in the Key Stage 3 Literacy Strategy and the Progress Units

Writing: Steps to Success draws on the established best practice of English teachers and on the model of teaching writing provided by the Key Stage 3 Literacy Strategy. All units follow a similar structure. Each unit begins with a description of the particular type of writing. It then establishes the features of the type of writing, in particular, the features of that type of writing at the level relevant to that book. Students have to assess their own skills in this type of writing and, through self-assessment, set themselves the targets that they need to reach to improve their writing from one level to the next. The description and self-assessment are followed by a series of activities which guide students through the planning and writing of a text. In each unit there is a set of activities clearly focused on developing the discrete skills necessary to write successfully at the target level, with emphasis on how to improve the complexity of their sentence writing. Throughout, students are encouraged to check their work to ensure that they have met the specific criteria for success. Each unit ends with further opportunities for students to write texts of that type. These opportunities are intended to move students from being dependent on the scaffolding provided by the book and their teacher, to being independent writers, with the requisite skills for successful writing internalised.

6   is designed to be used either with specific ability groups, in a mixed ability class, or with different year groups

The three books are not designed to be a replacement to existing schemes of work, but as a supplementary resource. If, as part of a scheme of work, a teacher wants to develop his or her students' expertise in a particular type of writing, the books provide detailed advice on how students can achieve such expertise. The books are not intended in any way to replace the teacher. Even though the activities are written with the students as the audience and are intended to help students develop skills independently, the role of the teacher is seen as essential, both in leading students through the process, and in providing opportunities to reinforce or clarify where necessary. The expertise of the teacher, therefore, is indispensable in deciding on pace, timing, groupings, and so on. It is assumed, also, that teachers will need to remind pupils of terminology, for example, clause, connective. Even at Level 3 to Level 4⁺, a growing familiarity with linguistic terms, and confidence in using and applying them, will enhance the capacity of students to develop independence as writers. It is not assumed, though, that the simple recitation of terms is of value; at all times, the identification of linguistic features should be related to their effect on meaning.

Obviously, each book is particularly focused on the needs of students at one level who need to move up to the next. However, the skills taught and practised in each unit will be relevant to a far wider group than just students at the lower level of each book. A student who has attained a certain level according to their test results may well still need to learn further key skills, in order to work confidently and consistently at the level identified. The activities, therefore, provide opportunities for students to achieve a more thorough grasp of the skills necessary for success at a particular level, or for them to consolidate skills only tentatively grasped. As a result, the books do not need to be restricted to a group where all students are at the target level.

There are probably three main ways in which the books can be used. In a mixed ability class, all three books could be used concurrently, with groups of different attainment using the book relevant to their level. In a setted environment, the book most relevant to the attainment of that group could be used. Alternatively, since each book uses the Framework Objectives for one of the years at Key Stage 3 as a starting point, a different book could be used with each of Years 7 to 9.

7 aims to keep the writing process real

While the books embody the belief that students need to be very clear about the criteria necessary for success, the authors are aware that writing should not become simply a menu of skills to be ticked off. Equally, with the demands of writing in such a wide range of types, there is the danger that the process is reduced simply to the speedy production of very short pieces of writing displaying a narrow set of skills. Aware of these dangers, the authors want to emphasise that each unit provides opportunities to produce a substantial text, with the process marked by the familiar stages of the writing journey, and its concern to shape meaning clearly and appropriately. Accordingly, students will plan, draft, check, redraft, and reflect, as they seek to produce writing that is lively and imaginative, committed and engaging.

Ultimately, the aim is to let students in on the secret of how to write effectively in a variety of text-types, and in so doing to give them more power and more control over what they do, thus guiding them on the road to being real and successful writers.

Students' Introduction

How can I improve my writing from Level 3 to Level 4[+]?

If you want to improve your writing, you need to know what features make a piece of writing Level 3. You also need to know the ways in which a Level 4 piece is better. These pages will give you an idea of what to look for.

Read the two pieces below. The writers had read a passage about Richard Branson and his attempts to fly around the world by balloon. They were then asked to carry out this task:

'Some people waste a lot of time and energy attempting difficult challenges, such as flying around the world in a hot-air balloon. Attempts like this are pointless and benefit nobody.'

Write an article for your local newspaper arguing <u>either</u> for <u>or</u> against this statement.

In your article you could:
- *explain which challenges you think are most worthwhile or pointless, and why*
- *say why you think people take part in challenges*
- *say which challenges, if any, you are interested in, and why*
- *end by summing up your views <u>either</u> for <u>or</u> against the statement.*

Text One

I think it is a pointless thing to do challenges which are no good to anybody, like flying, I think people should be doing challenges such as a fund-raising run around a town or place, in which everybody can join in if they want to. This is a challenge that people might do because it is helping raise money. My views toward doing pointless challenges are that they waste time and money and are not satisfying for many people.

Text Two

Do We Waste Time on Challenges?

To be truthful I am for the argument about wasting time and money trying to get around the world in a hot air balloon, when this time and money could be spent on helping people with medical difficulties or people who are homeless.

But there are some things that getting around the world in a balloon could be used for such as world records, entertainment and new transport.

I'd also say that people are taking part in this because they want to do something important and interesting, But on the other hand many people won't do ballooning as it's dangerous and expensive.

I think that I'd be interested in improving things in the world like medicine which I mentioned earlier, Instead of making more problems and things to improve.

To sum up my views I could positively say that I agree with the statement that challenges are a waste of time.

Discussion of texts

These pieces were both written under test conditions. There are, of course, many things that the writers would redraft if they could. However, Text One was graded as Level 3 and Text Two was given a Level 4. With a partner, discuss the questions below. They will help you think about why these pieces were graded like this. They will also suggest ways of improving Text Two.

Think about the task that was set. Discuss with your partner what the writers were being asked to do.

- Think about the **form** of writing asked for. Does either piece look or sound like a newspaper article?
- Think also about the **purpose** of the writing. This task asked for a **persuasive** piece, **arguing** a viewpoint. Do you feel that the writers are persuading you to agree with them? Do they build up their argument in a logical way?
- Think about the **audience** for the writing. Have these writers got a clear picture of who they are writing for?
- How far are these two writers doing what the task asked for? Look for words and phrases that give you clues.

Now look in more detail at sentence level.

- Do these writers use **full stops** and **capital letters** accurately? All the time, or some of the time?
- What about **commas**? Do they use commas to separate items in a **list**? To mark off **phrases** and **clauses** in a sentence? All the time, or some of the time?
- Does each writer change the **tense** of verbs without a good reason?
- When they write sentences with more than one clause, do they vary their sentences with **subordinate clauses**, **co-ordinate clauses**, or a **mixture** of the two?
- Do they write both long and short sentences, for **variety**?
- If they use **paragraphs**, does the first sentence of each one give an idea of the topic? Do the other sentences in the paragraph develop the **topic sentence** by **explaining** in more detail or by giving detailed **examples**?
- Do the writers link sentences and paragraphs with **connectives** to signpost the reader through the text?

What did you spot?

Now compare what you and your partner noticed with the points below. Look first at whole-text level:

- Probably the most important way to improve your writing level is to think carefully about the task set in a test or by your teacher. Think about the **form** of writing asked for. In these examples, the writers were asked for a newspaper article. Text One doesn't make any attempt to write like a newspaper article. Text Two has a headline, which could come from a newspaper. It also uses paragraphs, like a newspaper would. Both pieces use a first-person viewpoint (*I*) to put forward their ideas. This would be a feature of an opinion column, or perhaps a letter to a newspaper.
- The **purpose** of the writing is important. The writers are asked to **argue** a viewpoint. This means that they give reasons or examples, to **persuade** the reader that they are right. They also need to build up their argument in a logical way, again to persuade the reader. Text One gives some examples (*like flying, such as a fund-raising run*). It also gives a reason (*because*). However, these examples and reasons are not persuasive, because they are not developed. There is no feeling, either, that there is a logical structure to the argument, because the sentences don't seem to be connected. The argument isn't really clear, therefore. Text Two, in contrast, uses logical connectives such as *but, on the other hand, also, to sum up*. It also gives reasons (*because, as*) and examples (*such as*). These signposts for the reader help make Text Two easier to follow and more persuasive than Text One. However, Text Two would be even more persuasive if it had developed these examples and reasons further.
- Neither of these writers have got a clear picture of their **audience**. They don't sound as if they are aiming their writing at newspaper readers. The opening of Text Two sounds as if it is answering a question. It doesn't sound as if it is trying to capture a reader's attention and persuade them.
- Overall, Text Two follows the **instructions** in the task quite closely, whereas Text One only does so in a general way. However, Text Two doesn't really develop the ideas suggested by the bullet points. For example, while the third bullet point asks for reasons (*why*), in the third paragraph, the writer only says what he or she thinks, without explaining. Developing ideas would mean a more secure Level 4$^+$.

Look now in more detail at sentence level:

- Both writers can use **full stops** and **capital letters** accurately. But they don't get them right all the time. Accurate full stops and capital letters are essential for a sound Level 4⁺.

- Text One uses **commas** correctly to mark off one **phrase** and one **clause**. Text Two uses one comma in a **list**. The writer also uses commas to **separate clauses**, but sometimes follows the comma with a capital letter. Neither writer uses commas confidently. For a sound Level 4⁺, you need to show clearly that you understand how to use commas accurately. Commas help a reader follow more easily what you are saying.

- Both writers keep the **present tense** and don't change it without reason. For a sound Level 4⁺, you need to know the effect of verb tenses and when you use each tense.

- Text One uses a **co-ordinate clause** (*and are not satisfying . . .*). It also uses some **subordinators** (*which, in which,* and *that*). Text Two uses a couple of **co-ordinate clauses** starting with *but*. This writer, though, uses a much wider range of **subordinators**, such as *when, who, that, because, as, which*. Aim to use a wider range of **subordinate clauses** for a sound Level 4⁺. It will help you to say more, with a greater range of meaning.

- Neither writer varies the **length** of sentences. Even the writer of Text Two writes a series of long sentences. Shorter sentences would be useful to emphasise points, or to make points clear.

- Text One has no **paragraphs** – one big reason why it is not Level 4. Text Two organises points in **paragraphs**, but only has one sentence per paragraph. A sound Level 4⁺ would begin each paragraph with a **topic sentence**. It would also develop the **topic sentence** by **explaining** in more detail or by giving detailed **examples**.

- Text One doesn't help the reader with **connectives**. This is another reason why it is Level 3, not Level 4. Text Two uses some connectives, such as *also, on the other hand,* and *to sum up*. This helps give a logical structure to the argument. A good range of connectives is needed for a sound Level 4⁺.

Make a checklist

After you have discussed in detail the differences between these two texts, work with a partner to make a 'Level 4+ Checklist'. What things do you need to remember when you are trying to raise your writing from Level 3 to Level 4+? Make a list covering whole-text features and sentence features.

Note that your checklist will be a general one, giving an overall idea of what you need to aim at for Level 4+. In the units that follow, you will:

- look in detail at a range of writing types
- think about the features of each type of writing
- check your own writing against the features which you need to use
- track your improvements in the course of the unit.

Bear in mind that the examples which you have seen so far were written under test conditions. While you, too, will have to write under test conditions, most of your work at Key Stage 3 will be drafted. You can therefore develop ideas in detail, and work on getting punctuation correct. This book does not deal with spelling, but you must take care to check your spelling. You should also learn the spelling patterns which you know you find difficult. This will help you to achieve a sound Level 4+ in your writing.

Above all, keep checking. Each unit which follows will help you make a checklist of the writing features covered. If you have a checklist in your mind of the features which you should be including, you will be in control of what you are doing. And if you are in control, you will succeed. We wish you success with this process.

Unit One

Writing to imagine, explore, entertain

In this unit, you will:

- **think about what is special about writing to imagine, explore, entertain**

- **review your own writing, to see what needs to be done to make it a sound Level 4+**

- **look at how a professional author writes a short story to imagine, explore, entertain**

- **draft your own writing in this form.**

Main National Framework Objectives Covered: 7Sn1, 7Sn8, 7Wr1, 7Wr5, 8Sn1, 8Wr5, 9Wr5

Writing to imagine, explore, entertain – what is it?

This kind of writing describes an experience or an event, a person or a place. It might be about something that really happened, or it might be something made up by the writer. This kind of writing makes the reader imagine something, picture something, or feel something. If the writing describes an exciting event, it should make the reader imagine that they are there. If the writing describes a person, it should make the reader feel that they can see that person, and know what they are like.

● The writer should help the reader **imagine** what someone else's experience is like, or what a place is like.
● The writer should help the reader **explore** the thoughts and feelings of the characters in the writing.
● The reader should feel **entertained** and gripped by the writing, wanting to find out what happens to the people they are reading about.

Which of the following text-types do you think are meant to imagine, explore and entertain?

stories

diaries

advertisements

newspaper reports

autobiographies

poems

letters to friends

letters to local councils

jokes

science reports

Can you think of any other kinds of writing that are meant to imagine, explore and entertain?

What makes a good piece of writing to imagine, explore, entertain?

So how can you be successful as a writer, in helping your reader to picture what you describe, or in grabbing and holding their attention?

Here are some of the **features** of writing to imagine, explore and entertain.

In groups, put the following features in rank order. Which are the most important features in making a piece of writing successful? Why is each important? How will it help the reader?

- a good opening
- interesting characters
- detailed descriptions
- lots of action
- dialogue that helps us understand characters
- suspense, when we wonder how problems will be solved
- variety in the sentence structure
- accurate spelling, punctuation and paragraphing.

Compare your list with the lists made by other people. Do other groups agree with your rank order? Why? Work with your teacher to make a whole-class rank order, with reasons, of the features which a successful piece of writing to imagine, explore and entertain should have. Write your final list, with the reasons, into your notebook.

How can you improve your own writing?

Collect two or three pieces of your own writing to imagine, explore and entertain. Talk to your partner about the features you have been discussing. Some things you will be doing already. What things do you need to improve?

On this and the following page, there are grids which show in detail the things you need to do for a sound Level 4[+]. There are a lot of things to think about, but don't worry. A lot of them you will already be good at, but some you will need to improve. The grids will help you think about them. If you are not sure about a feature, your teacher will be able to explain. You could also wait to see how the feature is used later in the unit.

Copy the grids into your notebook. (It may also be possible for your teacher to photocopy them.) For each feature, put a tick in the box which applies to you. When you have finished, you will be able to see what you need to focus on in the rest of this unit. You can then go on to produce your own writing to imagine, explore and entertain, from page 6 onwards.

FEATURES OF WRITING	I can do this sometimes	I can usually do this	I need to improve this
I start my writing in a way that interests my reader.			
I give the reader clues suggesting problems or complications that might be developed later.			
I give details about characters' thoughts and feelings.			
I describe people and places in detail by expanding nouns into noun phrases.			
I keep the same verb tense throughout.			
I expand verbs with adverbial phrases.			
I use comparisons and metaphors.			
I keep the narrator's viewpoint clear, without changing who is telling the story.			

FEATURES OF WRITING	I can do this sometimes	I can usually do this	I need to improve this
I make sure that it is clear what each pronoun refers back to.			
I end sentences with a full stop.			
I start sentences with a capital letter.			
I write names with a capital letter.			
I write short sentences for effect.			
I write longer sentences for description.			
I separate subordinate clauses from main clauses with commas.			
I use a range of connectives to begin subordinate clauses.			
I start a new paragraph when I change topic.			
I start a new paragraph when I change time.			
I start a new paragraph when I change the speaker.			
I keep a list of the spellings and spelling patterns that I have trouble with.			
I check my drafts carefully for the spellings and patterns I have trouble with.			

Now that you have reviewed your writing, record in your notebook the main things that you need to work on and improve. Keep checking your progress throughout the unit.

Getting started: finding ideas to write about

There are many ways of writing to imagine, explore and entertain. The activities at the end of this unit will give you ideas about different forms in which you could write. In this section, though, we will concentrate on story-writing (**narrative** writing).

You can write stories about things that have happened to you. These are called **autobiographical stories**. They can be very entertaining to read. The reader can imagine what you did, and what your thoughts and feelings were. You can also write **fictional (made-up) stories**. You need to imagine the place where the story is set. You also need to imagine the characters in the story. You need to describe what they do, what they think and what they feel.

 To help you get started, try some think-writing in your journal. Just write down your thoughts for five or ten minutes, aiming to write as much as possible. Keep writing and don't stop. You can sort out the best ideas afterwards. You might find it useful to write only on the left-hand page of your notebook. This will give you room to redraft and add notes. Try some or all of the following activities:

- Write a **memory chain**. Write down a word, a phrase or a short sentence, summing up a memory that comes into your mind. Then add another memory which the first one makes you think of. Then add a third, and so on. See how many you can think of in five minutes. When you have finished your memory chain, pick one or two memories to write more about. Which ones would be most interesting to explore in more detail? Could you use them in autobiographical writing? Could you use them in a fictional story?
- **Picture** a place in your mind. Try to see the place clearly, as if you were watching a video. Describe this place – the shapes and colours, for example. Describe what things would feel like if you touched them. What sounds can you hear? Is this place inside or outside? Describe the light or the weather.
  - Is anyone in your scene? If there isn't, imagine someone walking in. Make sure you can see one, two or three people in your scene. Describe three or four things about each person. What do they look like? How do they move? What sort of people are they? Try to imagine their thoughts, or some things that they say. Write down their thoughts or speech.
  - Where does this scene come in your story? Is it from the beginning, the middle or the end? How do you know? Write your thoughts in your journal.
  - These notes will help get you started with your story. Swap journals with a partner. Ask them to underline five things that help them to imagine the place or the people. Ask them to put a ring round two things that aren't clear. You can do the same for your partner.

Planning your story

You have now got some ideas to work on. You will need to plan the overall shape of your story. Planning will make it easier to write. Copy the planning chart below into your notebook, and fill in the bullet points.

BEGINNING (OPENING)

The beginning sets the scene, introduces the characters and catches the reader's attention. Give the characters names. Use the bullet points to note down key pieces of information about characters and setting. Put in a clue to a problem for later on.

-
-
-
-

MIDDLE (DEVELOPMENT or COMPLICATION)

The middle develops the story by making it more complicated, or by raising problems for the characters to solve. This makes it entertaining for the reader. Note down between two and four complications or problems for the characters in your opening.

-
-
-
-

ENDING (CRISIS and RESOLUTION)

The ending brings the story to a crisis. It then solves the problems or sorts out the complications. It ties up the threads in the story. Note down what your crisis will be. Then add two or three ways to solve your problems or complications.

-
-
-
-

The opening of your writing

The opening of any narrative is important. The following extract is the beginning of *Tom Fobble's Day* by Alan Garner. The story is set during the Second World War. William, the main character, is sledging on Lizzie Leah's, a steep hill near his home. Stewart Allman is the local bully. ('Tom Fobble's Day' is what the local children shout when they are claiming something as their own.)

'Tom Fobble's Day!'

The first snowball caught William in the teeth. The second burst on his forehead, the third on his balaclava helmet.

He let go of his sledge and ran, blindly. The snowballs kept hitting him, on the back, on the legs, softly, quietly, but he couldn't stand them.

The snow gathered between the iron of his clogs and the curved wood of the sole and built into rockers of ice. His ankles twisted and he fell over, trying not to cry. He curled himself against the attack.

But it had stopped. He opened his eyes. He wasn't even out of range. Stewart Allman had stopped throwing and was sitting on William's sledge.

William stood up. 'Give us me sledge!' It had taken him a day and a morning to build it out of an old crate.

'It isn't yours,' said Stewart Allman.

'It is!'

'It isn't. I've Tom Fobbled it.'

Focus on the following points:

Effect on the reader:
The writer entertains the reader by starting the story in a dramatic way. He includes some speech, and some action, to get the reader involved.

Characters and setting:
He also includes some description of thoughts and feelings, and some description of the place. This helps us imagine what William and Stewart are like as people.

Choice of verbs:
The verbs he chooses help us imagine what the characters do, and what happens to them. *Caught* and *burst* help us see how the snowballs hit William.

Tenses of verbs:
Stories usually use the past tense all the way through, except for the dialogue.

Choice of adverbials:
Adverbials help us imagine where, when, why and how things happen. (For example, *in the teeth, blindly, trying not to cry*.)

Viewpoint:
Narratives are usually told in the first person (*I/we*) or the third person (*she/he/they*). Alan Garner uses a third-person viewpoint.

Sentences:
The sentences here are mainly on their own, or joined together by *but* or *and*. You will learn to use other connectives in this unit.

Punctuation:
Alan Garner uses four different punctuation marks. Count how many times he uses each one. Remind yourselves of the rules for using each of these punctuation marks.

It's your turn

You are now going to draft the opening to your own story.

Think back. Before you start, remind yourself of your personal targets from page xiii and 5. Remind yourself also of your story plan. Your opening should be between eight and ten sentences long. It should have:

* **a dramatic start.** (Include action and some speech.)
* **characters and setting.** (Include information about people and place.)

When you have finished, ask a partner to read your beginning over with you. Is the start dramatic, with action and some speech? Have you given enough information about people and place?

Now check that you have included:

* **first or third-person viewpoint** all the way through.
* **past tense** all the way through for the narrative. Don't mix tenses.
* **verb choice.** Pick five verbs and use a thesaurus to see if you can choose better verbs to describe the actions.
* **adverbials.** Include at least five **adverbial phrases**.

Alan Garner uses this pattern:

Preposition	Determiner	Noun
in	*the*	*teeth*
on	*his*	*forehead*
against	*the*	*attacks*

Now you do the same. Copy this table. Choose a word from the first column, one from the second, and put your own word into the third column.

Preposition	Determiner	Noun
Choose one of these: e.g. *in / on / under / against / out of*	Choose one of these: e.g. *the / a / her / his / their / our / your / my*	Put in your own word, here:

See if you can put into your story the five adverbials you have just written. They will tell the reader how, where, when or why things are happening. You can include more adverbials if you want.

Also check **sentences** and **punctuation**:

* **sentences and punctuation.** Keep your sentences quite short. Don't use more than two *ands* to connect the parts of each sentence. In your paragraph, use at least one sentence in which *but* connects sentence parts. This will give variety. Check that each sentence ends with a full stop.

Review. When you have improved your paragraph, spend a few minutes think-writing in your notebook. How have you made progress towards your targets?

More about people or places

In your story, you will need to give the reader more information about people or places. The next two pages will help you with writing descriptions. Here are two more extracts from *Tom Fobble's Day*. The first describes the hill where William and Stewart Allman are sledging. Read the extract and sketch what you can see in your mind.

Lizzie Leah's was the place where everybody went to sledge. It was two fields, one above the other and above the road. The bottom field was short and steep, and all that had to be done was to stop before the thorn hedge. The top field was long, and there was a gate in the corner to the bottom field.

Look at the way Alan Garner, the writer, gives information in sentences.

Subject	Verb	Phrase	Extra Information
The bottom field	*was*	*short and steep*	
The top field	*was*	*long*	
Lizzie Leah's	*was*	*the place*	*where everybody went to sledge.*
It	*was*	*two fields,*	*one above the other and above the road.*
There	*was*	*a gate*	*in the corner to the bottom field.*

Now you try this pattern. Picture in your mind the place where your story is set. Write four sentences describing it. Write two sentences with subject, verb and a phrase which describes the subject (like the first two examples). Write two where you give extra information about the phrase, which describes the subject (like the last three examples). This will help you vary your sentences.

Other ways to give extra information

The extract below comes after Stewart Allman has broken William's sledge. Afterwards, William visits his grandfather, who is a blacksmith. His grandfather's forge is in the cellar of a shop. William is standing outside the shop, on the iron grid which lets light into the cellar. Again, read the extract and sketch what you can see.

William stood on the grid. He could see Grandad's bench below, and the silver gleam of his hair.
William sniffed the drop off his nose. He was cold. He dragged his feet sideways across the grating, to free his clogs, but all he did was to push loose snow onto Grandad's window.
'Oh, flipping heck,' said William.
He had been watching the silver of Grandad's hair; now he was looking at his blue eyes and sharp red nose.
He went into the empty shop. The bell tinkled on its curled spring.
At the back of the shop there was a yard door that slid in grooves. William could open it with one finger, because Grandad had made a lead counterweight and hung it by a sashcord, so that the door was balanced. Behind the big, green door was the farrier's yard, where horses used to be shod, and from the yard broad steps went down to Grandad's cellar and forge and the flat, square cobbles.

Sashcord: rope that holds up the sash windows of old houses
Farrier: someone who shoes horses

When you've read this extract, think about how Alan Garner tells us a lot about Grandad through the details he gives us. We know what sort of age he is. We know that he is a very good blacksmith. We also know that William is just a little afraid of him. Can you find the details that tell us?

Now look at the way in which Alan Garner expands noun phrases with adjectives:

NOUN PHRASES		
Determiners	**Adjectives**	**Nouns**
the	*silver*	*gleam*
his	*blue*	*eyes*
the	*empty*	*shop*
its	*curled*	*spring*
the	*big, green*	*door*
the	*flat, square*	*cobbles*

Giving more information like this helps a reader to imagine what the writer is describing. You try it. (You might like to use a thesaurus to help you.) Picture your place or one of your characters. Try to make your reader see some of the details in your mind. Write three noun phrases with one adjective, and two noun phrases with two adjectives. Remember the comma, when you use two adjectives!

It's your turn

When you have tried out these two ways of giving extra information, use what you have written in a paragraph leading on from your opening. Tell the reader more about the setting of your story, or about the characters in it. Keep a picture of the setting or the people in your mind.

Review how this has helped you work towards your targets for improvement.

The middle of your story

Remember that the middle of a story develops the action by making it more complicated. It may raise problems for the characters to solve. The opening of *Tom Fobble's Day* shows us that William has a problem with Stewart Allman, who is the local bully. Stewart has also broken William's sledge, which is another problem. What questions does this put into your mind, to catch your interest?

 It's also William's grandfather's last day as a blacksmith, after fifty-five years. The last thing he does in his forge is to make William a new sledge, and William helps him. Grandfather uses wood and iron from his forge, and from the old weaver's loom which had belonged to his own grandfather. How might these details make the story more complicated, and build up suspense?

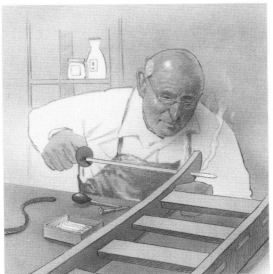

In the extract from the story which follows on the next page, William's grandfather is finishing off the new sledge. Where does the writer remind us of the problems from earlier in the story? What does William's grandfather think about these problems? What is the question which the writer has now put in the reader's mind and how will we find out the answer?

He examined the poker. 'Keep him that colour,' he said. He opened the corner cupboard above his chair. It was full of string and rope. He chose a length of rope, sashcord, like the sashcord that held the counterweight of the yard door above the cellar.

Grandad spat on the poker, tested its whiteness with his thumb, pressed it against the upcurve of one of the runners. The wood hissed and smoked, and the poker sank through. When it cooled, Grandad reheated it and pressed again. The room was full of the sweet smell of ash. There was a hole in the curve, like a black-rimmed eye.

Grandad burnt through the other runner, threaded the cord into both eyes, knotted the ends, and the sledge was complete.

'Is that for me?' said William, not daring to.

'Well, it's not for me!' said Grandad.

'For me own? For me very liggy own?'

'Ay. Get that up Lizzie Leah's and see what Allman's have to say. Loom and forge.'

It's your turn

You're now going to draft the middle section of your story. In it, you will develop the complications or problems from the opening. Write between four and six paragraphs, including at least two 'talk' paragraphs.

Think back. Before you start, remind yourself of your personal targets, and your plan (page 7). You could also remind yourself of how Alan Garner writes in this extract. Can you find:

- three examples of well-chosen **verbs**?
- two examples of **adverbials** that tell you where or how something happened?
- one example of an **expanded noun phrase** which gives a good description?

There are new things in this extract, as well. Look at:

- The **comparison** in *There was a hole in the curve, like a black-rimmed eye.*
  - What is Alan Garner describing here? In your notebook, draw a quick sketch of what he wants you to see. How are these two things similar? What is the effect of this comparison?
  - When you draft your middle section, make sure that you include at least one comparison.
- The range of **connectives** which Alan Garner uses.
  - In four sentences, he uses *and* to link clauses. Find the sentences and explain why *and* is the right connective to use. What do you notice about the commas?
  - When you draft your own middle section, don't overuse *and*. Use it like Alan Garner does. He usually writes only one *and* clause to a sentence. You should do the same, if possible. Remember to put a comma before the *and* clause, to separate it from the main clause.
  - He also uses *when* to begin a subordinate clause. What do you notice about where the subordinate clause comes in this sentence? List five other connectives which start subordinate clauses. When you draft your middle section, try to include these five connectives. Try to put the subordinate clause first in at least two sentences. Remember where the comma goes!
- The **paragraphs**. There are seven paragraphs in this extract. With a partner, look at each one and decide whether it shows a change of topic, a change of time, or a change of speaker (topic/time/talk).
  - Look at the punctuation marks Alan Garner uses for speech. List them all, and count how many times he uses each one. What are the rules for using each one? What rule do you notice for capital letters?
  - When you write your own middle section, try to vary punctuation. Include at least one question mark and at least one exclamation mark. Make sure that you put in all speech marks, commas, full stops and capital letters. Check whether each of your paragraphs shows a change of time, topic or speaker.

Now **review** what progress you have made towards your targets.

How to end your story

The final extract from *Tom Fobble's Day* comes from near the end of the story. William has climbed right to the top of Lizzie Leah's two fields with his new sledge. The long top field drops down to the hump and the gate to the steep lower field, which ends at the hedge. The other sledges are a long way below William. Stewart Allman and the other children are waiting for William to make his first run. Will he be successful? Will his new sledge work well?

William sat astride, his heels braced. He let out the rope, lay back, and eased the pressure off his heels. He felt the sledge start, and then he felt no speed, only a rhythm of the hill. The sledge found its own course; a touch corrected it. As he went faster, William used his clogs for balance. The steering moved into his hands and arms, then his shoulders, and then he was going so fast and so true that he could steer with a turn of his head.

The watching groups were a flicker as he passed, and his speed grew on the more trampled snow.

He saw the hump and the gate, but saw nothing to fear. He took in more rope, gripped, and the forge bellows runners breasted the air without shock. He pulled on the rope and kiltered his head to the right. His weight had brought him forward and the curved runners were at his shoulder. Then the trailing corners of the loom iron took the weight, the front of the sledge dropped away, and William was lying back again, coasting along the bottom field.

He put down his heels and stopped at the hedge.

Stewart Allman arrived.

'Any bones broken?' he said.

'No,' said William.

'We thought you'd be killed.'

'Get off with you!' said William. 'It's dead safe. Me Grandad made it.'

'Will you go again?' said Stewart Allman. 'From the top.'

'It's a heck of a climb,' said William.

'I'll give you a pull to half way,' said Stewart Allman.

'What about your sledge?'

'It's no weight. Honest. Will you?'

'OK.'

It's your turn

You're now going to draft the ending of your story. Remember that the ending brings the story to a crisis. It then solves the problems from the beginning and middle of the story. Alan Garner brings the story to a crisis with William at the top of the hill, ready to try out his new sledge. Alan Garner also solves William's problems from earlier in the story. First, Stewart Allman is the local bully. By the end of this extract, we can see that Stewart's attitude to William has changed. How does the writer show this change? What has caused the change? How do we, the readers, feel about it?

Second, Stewart broke William's first sledge. This second problem is solved when William's grandfather makes William a new sledge. But we still wonder if the sledge will work. The crisis in this extract shows us that it does. Alan Garner reminds us of how Grandad made the sledge, by including references to three objects that Grandad used. One thing is the rope he chose from his cupboard. Can you find the other two? Alan Garner perhaps uses these three things to suggest a 'message' or a moral in the story. Discuss what you think that the 'message' might be. (Look at what Grandad says on page 14.) How does it make the readers feel?

Think back. Before you begin writing, look back at your plan and at the earlier parts of your story. What is your crisis? Look also for characters who change during the story. Think about how they change, and why. How can you show this to the reader? By what the character does? By what he or she says? To help you record your ideas, draw the following chart into your notebook, and fill them in.

Name of character	How he or she changes	Why he or she changes	How I can show this

Look also for important objects which you could refer to at the end, like Alan Garner does. Draw this chart, and fill it in.

Important objects	Why they are important	How I can work them into the story

Now talk to your partner about your ideas for the ending. Would your ideas make a satisfying ending, solving the problems and rounding everything off? When you think you've got your ideas sorted out, draft the ending. Write four to six paragraphs. Include some dialogue. Remember to use what you've learnt from earlier in your story, for example: expanding noun phrases; using adverbials; writing short sentences for effect; not using more than one *and* clause in a sentence; using a range of connectives. **Review** your progress towards your targets.

Revising your draft

When you've finished your draft, you'll need to revise it before you write your final version. First, ask a few people to read it over.

Ask them to tell you:

- What picture they had in their mind of the people and places in your story. (Did you help them **imagine** the people and places?)
- Whether your story reminded them of anything, made them think of anything, or gave them new ideas about anything. (Did you help them to **explore** thoughts, feelings or ideas?)
- What they enjoyed about your story. (Did it **entertain** them?)

Ask them also to tell you:

- What they liked about the way you wrote the story, for example, **sentence patterns** they thought were effective, **expanded noun phrases** or **adverbials** they thought were descriptive, **comparisons** or **metaphors** that made them see things in a new or fresh way.
- Whether they have any questions about things that aren't clear, or need explaining in more detail.
- Whether they have any ideas for improving parts of your story.

Make notes about improvements when you are collecting ideas for developing your draft. If you have written on the left-hand page only, make notes on the right-hand page. If not, you could make notes in the margin, or on Post-It notes which you stick into your notebook. This will help you when you write your final version.

Before you write your final version, check over the following features:

- Have you kept the same **verb tense** all the way through? (past tense for stories)
- Have you kept the same narrator's **viewpoint** all the way through? (first person or third person?)
- Are your **pronouns** clear? (Ask your partner to read your draft, highlighting each pronoun. If they aren't sure what the pronoun refers back to, they should put a question mark in the margin. You will then need to make it clear.)

And:

- Have you ended each sentence with a **full stop**? (Work with a partner. Count the number of sentences you have written in each paragraph. Write the number in the margin. Then count the number of full stops. The numbers should be the same!)
- Do all your sentences **begin with a capital letter**? (Underline the first word of each sentence. Has it got a capital letter?)
- Have you used **capital letters for names**? (Underline each name in your story. Put a ring round the first letter. Is it a capital?)
- Have you separated **subordinate clauses** from main clauses with **commas**? (Look at the start of each clause to see if it begins with a connective. If there is a connective, put a box around it. Where should the comma go?)
- Have you used a **range of connectives**? (Look at the connectives you have marked. If you have used more than one *and* clause in a sentence, is there a good reason? Have you used five other connectives, apart from *and* or *but*?)

And:

- Have you started a **new paragraph** when you change **topic, time or speaker**? (Read through your draft, and label each new paragraph as topic, time or talk. Do you need to join some paragraphs or to split others?)
- Have you checked the **punctuation of speech**? (Revise the rules. Put a ring round the speech marks that begin and end speech. Remember the comma and the capital letter. Where do they go?)

And finally:

- Check your draft carefully for the **spelling patterns** you know you have trouble with. (Use your spelling list to remind you.)

When you are ready, **review** your progress using the grids from pages 4 and 5. What features of writing have you improved? The more improvements you have made, the closer you are to a sound Level 4$^+$.

And you could try . . .

Here are a few extra ideas for writing to imagine, explore and entertain. You may like to try at least one of them. Use the techniques that you have been developing in this unit. Think about your individual targets for improvement, and work on them. Finally, think about presentation – not just handwriting, but whether you could use word-processing and illustrations to make your story look good. What about designing a cover and writing a blurb? What about getting it bound into a book? What about having a publisher's party, where your class brings in (not too messy!) food and drink? You could read each other's books, and write reviews, like the book reviews in newspapers and magazines. You will need to collect examples of these reviews, to see what reviewers say, and how they say it. You could make a wall display from the reviews written by your class.

- You could write about something that happened to you in the past. This is called autobiographical writing. It is normally written in the first person (*I/we*). Try writing it in the third person (*he/she/they*), as if you were writing a fictional story, and you were a character in it. Be careful with the narrator's viewpoint, though. It's easy to slip back into the first person. Remember to help the reader imagine people and places. Entertain the reader with a dramatic opening, an interesting development/complication, a crisis and an ending which solves problems in a satisfying way. You may need to change things that actually happened. Don't worry. Writers do it all the time!
- You may have heard some good stories about members of your family. Again, try writing the story as if your relative was the main character in a fictional story. Try to explore their thoughts and feelings, as well as helping the reader to imagine what they are like, and where the story is taking place. (You could read it to them, and see if they recognise who the story is about.)
- Try writing a story from an unusual narrative point of view – e.g. an animal, a tree, a baby, a car, an alien. (You may think of extra viewpoints to experiment with.) When you write, try to imagine how your narrator would see the world. What things would they notice or say? Would they speak to the reader directly, or make it seem as if the reader was overhearing their thoughts? Make your reader imagine what it is like to be that narrator. To entertain the reader, don't let them know who or what the narrator is, until right at the end. Keep it as a surprise.
- You might like to begin a story with the ending. For example, you could start with the main character looking back on what had happened, but not telling the reader a vital piece of information. The rest of the story then leads up to and explains the beginning. What would be the effect of that?
- Write a story, or a section from a story, from a genre such as science fiction, horror, romance, fantasy or historical novel. What are the ingredients for your chosen genre? Think about characters, speech and setting. This would be a good opportunity to concentrate on expanded noun phrases, adverbials, comparisons and metaphors, and sentence structures.

Unit Two

Writing to inform, explain, describe

In this unit, you will:

- think about what is special about writing to inform, explain, describe

- review your own writing, to see what needs to be done to make it a sound Level 4$^+$

- look at how professional authors write websites and guides to inform, explain, describe

- draft your own writing in this form.

Main National Framework Objectives Covered: 7Sn8, 7Wr10, 7Wr11, 8Wd10, 8Wd11, 8Sn7, 8Wr10, 9Sn2, 9Wr12

Writing to inform, explain, describe – what is it?

The majority of the writing you read in school (and out of school) is probably writing to **inform**, **explain** and **describe**. This writing covers a wide range of topics or subjects.

- Writing to **inform** gives you facts. It does not try to persuade you to follow one particular viewpoint or argument. For example, it may be writing you find in a Religious Studies textbook, such as *What is Buddhism*? You may find it on the Internet (e.g. when searching for information on *food suitable for hedgehogs*). You may also find it in a newspaper, for example, in an article entitled: *Ten outdoor activity summer holidays for teenagers*. It may be an advice leaflet from your doctor's surgery, about the signs and symptoms of meningitis. The writer tells us information so we may find out new facts. This writing usually answers the questions: Who? What? Where? When?

- Writing to **explain** helps to make something plain or clear to the reader. For example, the writing may be explaining why soil erosion occurs, or what happens to the food we eat. The writer is usually explaining processes or difficult ideas. They will give us many facts. There may be more than one explanation or reason for an event, though, so writers then pick the most important information for the reader. For example, if we think about why soil erosion occurs we may come up with several reasons. These reasons will form part of the explanation. Writing to explain usually answers the questions why and how.

- Writing to **describe** often combines information and explanation. The writer describes what happened during a particular time or event. For example, they could write a description of life in India during the rainy season. They could also write a description of what happened during the World Cup, including what a particular football team felt about the event. This writing may answer a range of questions (including who, what, when, where, why, or how), depending on what the writer chooses to focus on. The writer selects what details to put into their description. Of the three forms of writing, descriptive writing is most likely to include adjectives, imagery and descriptive detail. You will also find lots of examples of descriptive writing in fiction texts that you read.

There are several overlaps between these forms of writing. A leaflet about a disease such as malaria, for example, may include information about symptoms. It may also explain what to do if you think you have the disease. It may also describe different types of malaria and where they are found. This kind of writing is rarely pure information, explanation or description. It is usually a mixture of text-types, with features of all three types of writing.

Discuss the following text-types. Which ones are meant to inform, explain and describe? Which ones have a combination of these types of writing? Discuss the list and see what you think.

a newspaper article about how to help wild animals survive winter
a story about a refugee living in a refugee camp on the border of Afghanistan
a letter from a soldier fighting in World War One
'the story of a chip: what happens once it's eaten'
a science fiction story
a private diary entry
a description of life in a Brazilian rain forest
an explanation of how hot air balloons work
an encyclopaedia entry about walruses
an Internet site run by the 'Save the Dolphin' society
a leaflet entitled 'Drugs: their use and abuse'
an extract from a travel magazine about the Caribbean
an evaluation of your set design in Drama
a letter to the newspaper complaining about a new housing development
a leaflet from Greenpeace about why they are protesting against mining on the beaches
a journal entry entitled 'My trip to the North Pole – day 37'
an essay entitled 'The problems facing Zimbabwe'
an advertisement about a new shower gel
a letter about the new savings rates offered by a bank
a science experiment

What makes a good piece of writing to inform, explain, describe?

You now have an idea about the general features of writing to inform, explain and describe. You have also discussed some examples of these types of writing. For homework, collect as many different examples of these types of writing as you can. You will need to use a variety of sources to try and find as many different forms of this writing as possible. You could look in the following places:

- the Internet
- an encyclopaedia
- school text books (remember to look at writing in other subjects, not just English)
- newspapers and magazines
- free information leaflets (available in supermarkets, Tourist Information Centres, DIY shops, pharmacies, doctors' surgeries, and so on)
- writing you have done in a range of subjects.

 Working in groups, look at the examples you have collected. What **features** of writing to inform, explain and describe can you identify? Use your knowledge of non-fiction text-types to help you to identify key features at word, sentence and text level. Do you think that some of the group's examples are better than others? Can you explain why? Here are some ideas to help you to focus your discussion:

- Is there a heading that makes the **purpose** of the writing clear to the reader?
- Who is the **audience** for the writing? How do you know?
- How does the writer **catch our attention**?
- Is the writing easy to understand, with effective use of **connectives** to link ideas? Collect examples of different ways in which the writers connect their ideas.
- Are there **sub-headings** or **diagrams** to help us? How are these features helpful to the reader?

How can you improve your own writing?

Collect two or three pieces of your own writing to inform, explain and describe. Remember to look at writing in other subjects, as well as in English. Compare them with the two examples in the Students' Introduction. Talk to your partner about the things you do already. What things do you need to improve?

On this and the following page, there are grids which show in detail the things you need to do to achieve a sound Level 4^+. There are a lot of things to think about, but don't worry. A lot of them you will already be good at, but some you will need to improve on. The grids will help you think about which areas you need to improve. If you are not sure about a feature, your teacher will be able to explain. You could also wait to see how the feature is used later in the unit.

Copy the grids into your notebook. (It may also be possible for your teacher to photocopy them.) For each feature, put a tick in the box which applies to you. When you have finished, you will be able to see what you need to focus on in the rest of this unit. You will then be able to track your targets and improvements as you write.

FEATURES OF WRITING	I can do this sometimes	I can usually do this	I need to improve this
I capture the reader's interest with an effective heading.			
I focus on layout to make my text appealing, using diagrams, tables and illustrations, if appropriate.			
I write in a formal / impersonal or informal / personal style, as needed.			
I structure my writing to suit its purpose.			
I use a range of connectives to link my ideas.			
I explain clearly so that the reader understands what I am talking about.			
I select the amount of detail to use, for the purpose of my writing.			

FEATURES OF WRITING	I can do this sometimes	I can usually do this	I need to improve this
I start sentences with a capital letter.			
I end sentences with a full stop, question mark or exclamation mark.			
I write proper nouns (for example, names) with a capital letter.			
I use the third person to write in an impersonal style when needed.			
I select the correct verb tense to use and use it consistently.			
I write short sentences to explain my ideas clearly.			
I use connectives to link my ideas together and show the reader the relationship between my ideas.			
I divide my ideas into paragraphs.			
I start each paragraph with a topic sentence.			
I develop the topic sentence by giving examples or explaining in more detail.			
I use subordinate clauses to vary my sentences.			
I can use commas to separate subordinate clauses from the main clause, if needed.			
I can use specialist vocabulary to suit my topic and reader.			
I choose whether to write in a plain style or to include more detail and description.			
I keep a list of the spellings and spelling patterns that I have trouble with.			
I check my drafts carefully for the spellings and spelling patterns I have trouble with.			

 Now that you have reviewed your writing, record in your notebook the main things that you need to work on and improve. Keep checking your progress throughout the unit.

Online examples of writing to inform, explain, describe

You can get many texts to inform, explain and describe from the Internet. Consider the home page from this website.

The Severn Bore Page

Home
When
Where
Map
Application
9 Year Cycle
Facts
Factors
Photos
Videos
Sports
Links
Guestbook

Introduction

The bore at Lower Parting
LATEST NEWS
Times for 2002 are now available

"When the boar comes, the stream does not swell by degrees, as at other times, but rolls in with a head...foaming and roaring as though it were enraged by the opposition which it encounter" – Thomas Harrel 1824°

The Severn Bore is one of Britain's few truly spectacular natural phenomena.° It is a large surge wave that can be seen in the estuary of the River Severn, where the tidal range is the 2nd highest in the world, being as much as 50 feet (approx. 15.4m).*

As many as 60 bores occur throughout the world where the river estuary is the right shape and the tidal conditions are such that the wave is able to form. The Severn Bore (one of 8 in the UK) is one of the biggest in the world but bores also occur on the Seine and Gironde in France, on the Indus, Hooghly and Brahmaputra in India, on the Amazon in Brazil, on the Petitcodiac, New Brunswick, and also the Knik Arm bore at the head of Cook Inlet, Alaska. By far the biggest bore in the World is the Ch'ient'ang'kian (Hangchou-fe) in China. At spring tides the wave attains a height of up to 25 ft (7.5 m) and a speed of 13-15 knots (24-27 km/h). It is heard advancing at a range of 14 miles (22 km)*

The shape of the Severn estuary is such that the water is funnelled into an increasingly narrow channel as the tide rises, thus forming the large wave. The river's course takes it past Avonmouth where it is approximately 5 miles wide, then past Chepstow and Aust, then Lydney and Sharpness where it is approximately 1 mile wide, and soon the river is down to a width of a few hundred yards. By the time the river reaches Minsterworth it is less than a hundred yards across, maintaining this width all the way to Gloucester.†

As well as the width of the river decreasing rapidly, then so does the depth of the river also change rapidly, thereby forming a funnel shape. Therefore as the incoming tide travels up the estuary, it is routed into an ever decreasing channel. Consequently the surge wave or bore is formed.†

Note the following helpful features of the website:

- the contents of the website
- links to other sites
- a heading
- a quotation (from a writer in 1824) which sets the scene and creates atmosphere
- paragraphs which answer the following questions:
  What is the Severn Bore? (**Paragraph one**)
  How does it compare to other bores (surge waves)? (**Paragraph two**)
  Where and why does it occur? (**Paragraphs three and four**)

- the mixture of text-types. There are examples of information*, description°, and explanation†.
- the use of the present tense
- different spellings of *bore*. (What is a *boar*? Why do you think the different spellings were used? To help you, think about the different times during which these texts were written.)

- subject-specific vocabulary, for example: *tidal wave, estuary, knots*
- the formal, impersonal style, for example: *It is heard advancing at a range of 14 miles (22 km).*
- the connectives used to link the writer's ideas, for example: *as many as, by the time, therefore, consequently.*

It's your turn

Look again at the home page from the website and then discuss these questions with a partner or with a small group of your classmates.

- What is the main **purpose** of the website?
- Who is the **audience**? How do we know this?
- What sort of **information** does the website give you?
- Why has a **picture** been included?
- Would it have helped you if there had been **sub-headings**?
- Can you think of any other examples of **layout** and **organisation** that would add to the helpfulness of the website?
- The introductory quotation has been placed inside inverted commas or quotation marks. Why is this?
- Why has the author used the **present tense** to write the information?
- How much technical or **specialised vocabulary** has been used? How helpful are these terms for the reader?
- Pick out the **topic sentence** in each paragraph or section of the text.
- If you had to give the web page a rating out of 10 what would it be? Discuss the reasons for your rating with your partner or group. Focus on how well the examples in the paragraphs help to develop the topic sentences.

Now, as a group, come up with a checklist of features you need to include to have an effective web page. It may be helpful to categorise these as **essential** features (ones the web page must have) and **desirable** features (ones the web page could have).

Looking at one more example before you start your research and writing

The following extract is taken from *Getaway Adventure Guide*, a text published in South Africa.

Going Down Gorgeous

KLOOFING

While they're still in the mountains, rivers are young and exuberant. They hop, they skip, they jump. They leap over cliffs, sending spray skyward. They sulk in deep defiles like moody teenagers. They're not forthcoming, not easily approached, ridden and harnessed, like they are on the plains. But they're worth getting to know. It's a wild ride.

WHAT IT'S ALL ABOUT

Kloofing, called canyoning in most other parts of the world, is immense fun. It involves following a river through a deep mountainous gorge, or kloof. Obviously, some walking is involved, but the defining feature is that you get wet. Usually you have to boulder-hop, and jumping from high places into deep water and swimming is what it's all about. Abseiling is often a part of kloofing.

GETTING STARTED

Always go with someone who knows where they're going and what they're doing. Kloofing can be very dangerous, especially if you don't know the area. However, it really isn't very difficult, and you don't need special skills, just a bit of nerve and stamina. If you can't swim, you could use a lifejacket.

EQUIPMENT AND CLOTHING

The first thing to remember about kloofing is that you are going to get wet. Very wet. You may like to wear a thin wetsuit. Otherwise, if the weather's warm, you could get by in a swimsuit, light, synthetic shorts and a T-shirt. You can wear hiking boots, but they are difficult to swim in, and they will suffer. The best is a pair of those amphibious nylon-and-rubber sandals, or shoes specially designed for getting wet. Yes, you can buy special kloofing shoes – they're like running shoes but have a mesh section so the water drains out. Running shoes would also do, but they will be ruined if you do it too often.

The best way to carry your stuff is in waterproof packaging inside a day pack. Plastic bags will do for clothes and so-forth, but cameras, cellphones and the like should be kept in proper waterproof containers. Take a hat and sunscreen; it's easy to forget how strong the sun is when you are wet and cool. Sunglasses are more trouble than they're worth on most kloofs.

Now discuss what you like about the text with a partner or small group of your classmates. Note the following features that the author uses:

- alliterative heading that includes a pun: *Going Down Gorgeous*. This is clever as a gorge is a canyon, so *gorgeous* refers to the canyon they are climbing and the excitement of the activity.
- descriptive introductory paragraph which personifies rivers (describes rivers as though they are people and have personalities) and engages the reader
- informal language, such as *sunglasses are more trouble than they're worth*
- unconventional (unusual) sentence structures, such as the short sentence: *Very wet.* This is quite informal, to suit the style of writing, and to emphasise the state you will find yourself in.
- sub-headings to direct the reader's attention
- short paragraphs
- a definition or explanation of the topic
- clear language and explanations
- colloquial [chatty] tone that sounds as though the writer is talking directly to the reader: *Yes, you can buy special kloofing shoes . . .*
- instructions and information mixed together: *Always go with someone who knows where they're going and what they're doing. Kloofing can be very dangerous, especially if you don't know the area*
- descriptive detail, including adjectives and noun phrases
- technical, subject-specific vocabulary
- second-person pronouns which allow the writer to talk directly to the reader
- present tense.

It's your turn

You are now going to research a topic and then draft your own writing to inform, explain and describe. You could write your own home page for a website (or an entry for a non-fiction book). You could write about any topic that interests you.

Choosing a topic

Think about a particular interest you have. You could also do some extra research to support your work in another subject you are studying at the moment. You will use a combination of writing to inform, explain and describe.

Here are some ideas to help you:

- Research an interesting natural event, such as the Internet example about the Severn Bore. Topics could include volcanoes, earthquakes, floods, dust devils, heated springs, or any other natural occurrence. You need to explain what it is, why it occurs, and what happens during the event / process.
- Research an unusual animal. It could be an animal from your country or from another country. Think about interesting features of that animal that people would want to find out about. To help you to select a topic, think about animals you may have seen on television documentaries or wildlife programmes. You need to describe unusual features of the animal, explain what threats to its existence there are, how it survives, and why people are fascinated by it.
- Research an unusual sport or hobby, such as the example already given about kloofing, also known as canyoning. You could investigate any sport you are interested in. Alternatively, you could research one of the popular adventure sports, such as skydiving, wild water rafting, snowboarding, or bungee jumping. Think about what attracts people to unusual and possibly dangerous activities such as these. You need to explain what the sport is, what equipment is involved, where it happens, and why people are interested in it.

Before you start your research you need to think carefully about possible topics. What topic interests you? Think of two or three possible topics before you make your final selection. Try your ideas out on your friends. Which ideas do they think are interesting? It is best to check whether your teacher thinks you have chosen a suitable topic before you start your research.

Researching your topic

Before you start your research, remember your **purpose** (to write a text which will inform, explain and describe an interesting topic) and your **audience** (secondary school pupils).

Now consider the following points:

- **Where will you find your information?** List at least five different sources of information you could use.
- **What questions do you wish to find answers for?** Think about questions that ask who, what, where, when, why and how. Write down at least five questions that you will answer, each starting with a different questioning word. You will probably think of other questions to answer when you start your research. However, it's a good idea to have a clear aim in mind before you start looking for information. This will help you to focus your research.
- **What note-making skills will you need to use?** Remember to only write down key words or phrases so that you don't copy information straight from the original text.

Now you need to research your topic, finding the answers to the questions you set yourself at the beginning of this unit.

Planning and writing your draft

When you have collected your ideas, you need to start to plan and then write your first draft. Think about:

- **The purpose of your writing.** Remember you are going to give a combination of information, explanation and description. Think carefully of the balance between these three types of writing. How much information, explanation and description do you need to help your reader to understand and enjoy your topic? To help you to do this, write your draft and then highlight each of the different types of writing in a different colour.

- **Your audience.** You will be writing for secondary school pupils who are the same age as you.

- **Where your writing will be published.** Is it intended for a website or a text book? If you haven't yet created a web page, this may be a good opportunity to do so now. You can use the model you have seen in this book and examples you have found from your own research to help you decide how best to do this. If you are going to write an extract for a text book, use the example given earlier on kloofing and examples from your school text books as models to help you.

- **The formality of your writing.** This depends on your topic, but generally you write in a formal style when you are writing to inform, explain or describe. This will help your readers to take your views seriously. You may find it useful to use second person pronouns, such as *you* and *your*, to help draw your reader into your subject more closely.

- **The layout of your text.** Think about using features such as headings, sub-headings, pictures, diagrams or charts. They will help your readers to follow what you are saying.

It is a good idea to draw a flowchart or rough sketch, like the example you are given on page 35 of this unit, showing how your ideas link together. Your flowchart should contain an overview of the layout of your text, plus the headings for the different sections you will include.

A flowchart of your draft

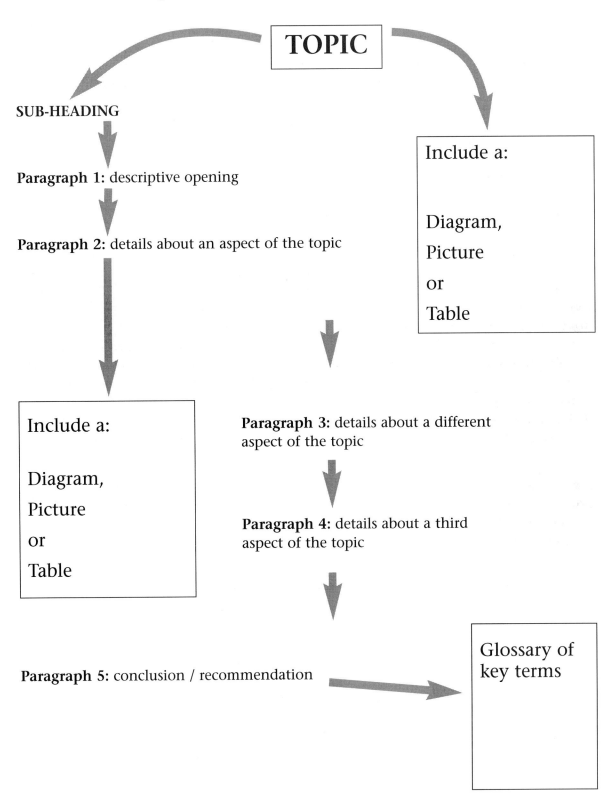

TOPIC

SUB-HEADING

Paragraph 1: descriptive opening

Paragraph 2: details about an aspect of the topic

Include a:

Diagram,

Picture

or

Table

Include a:

Diagram,

Picture

or

Table

Paragraph 3: details about a different aspect of the topic

Paragraph 4: details about a third aspect of the topic

Paragraph 5: conclusion / recommendation

Glossary of key terms

A descriptive opening

You could start your writing with a descriptive sentence or paragraph to engage your reader's attention. In pairs or small groups, look again at the opening quotation of the Severn Bore web page:

'When the boar comes, the stream does not swell by degrees, as at other times, but rolls in with a head ... foaming and roaring as though it were enraged by the opposition which it encounter'

- What does this description make you think of?
- What is the water being compared to?
- What powerful words have been used to create this image?
- Why did the author start with this description? How does it add to the rest of the extract?

Look again at the opening paragraph to the kloofing (canyoning) extract. As in the previous account, water has again been made to seem like a person:

While they're still in the mountains, rivers are young and exuberant. They hop, they skip, they jump. They leap over cliffs, sending spray skyward. They sulk in deep defiles like moody teenagers. They're not forthcoming, not easily approached, ridden and harnessed, like they are on the plains. But they're worth getting to know. It's a wild ride.

- Here the author compares rivers to several living things. Pick out three of these.
- How do these images help you to understand what the author says about rivers?
- Which particular words are the most powerful?
- Why did the author start with a descriptive paragraph like this? How does it add to the rest of the extract?

Now write the opening paragraph for your text. Write about three sentences. Remind yourself of your plan. Think about an opening sentence which captures the reader's attention and prepares them for the rest of the text. You might try:
  - a descriptive opening
  - describing things as if they were people
  - speaking directly to the reader.

Organising your ideas into paragraphs

You should aim to have at least **five paragraphs** in your writing. You have already written the first paragraph, your descriptive, introductory paragraph. The second, third and fourth paragraphs need to explain different features of your topic. Your final paragraph should be your conclusion or recommendation, summing up your interest in your chosen topic.

You can organise paragraphs in non-fiction texts in different ways. Here are some examples of how to organise your paragraphs:

In order of time (chronology):

the background to the French Revolution (events before 1789)
the events during the weeks leading up to the revolution
what happened next (the next few weeks)
the next six years
the importance for the French people.

In order of importance:

introduction
the most important reason
the second most significant reason
the third most significant reason
other minor reasons
conclusion.

In order of logic or the 'best fit' for the ideas:

what it is / what it looks like
where it is found (and why)
special features for survival
the food it eats
how it breeds
problems facing the young.

 Before you continue, **review** the plan of your writing that you have completed. How have you organised your ideas? Is this the 'best fit' for your topic? Are there any paragraphs that could be moved elsewhere? Is your second choice a better position for them, or do you prefer your first choice?

Topic sentences

For each of your paragraph headings, now write an effective topic sentence. It needs to introduce clearly the main idea you will expand on in your paragraphs.

When you write the remainder of your paragraph, remember to develop the idea in your topic sentence. You need to give more detail and add examples. Write your remaining four paragraphs now. In the margin of your draft, identify whether you have given more details or added examples. Write **D** (for detail) or **E** (for examples) in the margin.

Varying your nouns or noun phrases

Now think of different ways in which you could describe the subject of your sentence. You could match the noun phrases you use to the pictures you wish to create in your reader's mind. For example, if you are writing about **tidal waves**, you could start your sentences with:

- *Tidal waves . . .*
- These *giant waves . . .*
- *Walls of water* like these . . .
- *Leviathan monsters . . .* (Leviathan means something of enormous size and power; it is named after a sea monster in the bible.)
- *Towering mountains of water . . .*

Discuss with your partner what the difference is between using noun phrases like these and repeating the same topic or subject.

 Before you continue, try to write down at least three different nouns or noun phrases you could use to write about your chosen topic. Ask a partner whether the noun phrases you have chosen match the images you want to create in your reader's mind.

Sentence structure

Look again at your topic sentences. Try to vary the way in which you structure your topic sentences, so that you do not always start with the noun or noun phrase.

Look at these examples:

● You could start with an **adverb**.

Always *go with someone who knows where they're going and what they're doing.*
Certainly *safety should be your major focus.*

● You could start with a **subordinate clause**.

_When the drought is over_*, the animals migrate back to the plains in the north.*
_If you want to attract wildlife to your garden_*, leave wild areas and avoid tidying up too much.*
_Although many horse trails are suitable for beginners_*, you will be more comfortable and confident if you have some horse-riding experience.*

Discuss with your partner what difference it would make if the underlined part of each sentence had not been included.

For each of the sub-headings you've given in your plan, write an effective topic sentence. Remember to start several of your topic sentences with an adverb or with a subordinate clause. Think about how the way in which you have started your sentence adds to what you have to say.

Using connectives and connective phrases to join your ideas

In non-fiction writing, the links between your sentences are very important. For example, when explaining a process to your reader, you need to think about the connections between your sentences.

Look at these examples:

- *<u>If you can't swim</u>, you could always use a lifejacket.*
- *<u>Therefore</u>, as the incoming tide travels up the estuary, it is routed into an ever-decreasing channel.*
- *<u>For this reason</u>, many people believe it is important to protect wild animals.*
- *<u>A further point to consider</u> is whether you wish to spend lots of money on equipment.*

Look at the words and phrases which are underlined. Discuss with a partner what each of these words or phrases tells the reader.

Remember to use a range of connecting phrases to link your ideas. Some more examples you may wish to try are included below:

To add ideas to a list of points:

A further example is . . .
Additionally,
Another reason is . . .
Similarly,
As well as

To give a different point of view:

Alternatively,
On the other hand
Despite this
A different viewpoint is . . .

To explain relationships:

If . . .   then . . .
As . . .   so . . .
This results in . . .
As a consequence
Because

Use at least one of these examples for each of your paragraphs. Now underline the connective you have used in each paragraph. Before you continue, re-read your work and check whether the links between your ideas are clear.

Layout and presentational features

This is the final aspect for you to consider before you present your research. Think carefully about how to make your research easy for your reader to understand. What features of layout or presentation would help them? Go back to the checklist you made earlier in the chapter and see which of those features you will include in your work. You may like to consider some of the following ideas, but remember that you do not have to include them all. Only select features that will help your reader.

- headings and sub-headings
- different size fonts
- bold font for key words or specialised terms
- bullet points or numbered ideas
- short paragraphs
- diagrams, tables, charts, flow-charts
- a glossary.

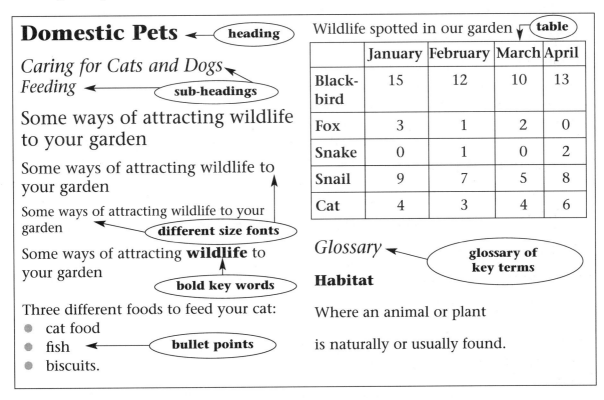

Are there any other features you could use? Think of the research you have done in preparation for this project. What features helped you most?

Now use at least three presentational features to make your work easier for your reader to understand.

Revising your drafts

When you've finished your drafts, work with a partner to revise some or all of them before you write your final version.

Check over the following features:

- Is it **clear** what you have said? Ask your partner to read your drafts. Ask them to mark places where they aren't sure what you mean. Ask them to mark places where the sentences don't follow on clearly.
- Have you used the right **verb tenses**? (Mainly present tense.)
- Are your **pronouns** clear? (Ask your partner to read your drafts, highlighting each pronoun. If they aren't sure what the pronoun refers back to, they should put a question mark in the margin. You will then need to make it clear.)

And:

- Have you ended each sentence with a **full stop**? (Work with a partner. Count the number of sentences you have written in each paragraph. Write the number in the margin. Then count the number of full stops. The numbers should be the same!)
- Do all your sentences **begin with a capital letter**? (Underline the first word of each sentence. Has it got a capital letter?)
- Have you used **capital letters for names**?
- Have you separated some of your **subordinate clauses** from main clauses with **commas**? (Look at the start of each clause to see if it begins with a connective. If there is a connective, put a box around it. Do you need to use a comma?)
- Have you used a **range of connectives**? (Look at the connectives you have marked. Don't overuse *and* or *but*. Have you used most of the connectives you have learnt in this unit? List them and check.)

And:

- Have you used a **topic sentence** when you start a new paragraph? (Underline the topic sentence in each paragraph.)
- Have you **developed** the topic sentence in the rest of the paragraph? (Mark the following sentences with 'explain' or 'example'. This will help you see how each sentence develops the topic sentence.)

And finally:

- Check your drafts carefully for the **spelling patterns** you know you have trouble with. (Use your spelling list to remind you.)

When you are ready, **review** your progress using the grids from pages 25 and 26. What features of writing have you improved? The more improvements you have made, the closer you are to a sound Level 4[+].

And you could try . . .

● Write a leaflet for your school to give to new Year 7 pupils, which explains what pupils can do if they experience any bullying. Try to make your tone as reassuring as possible. Write simple, clear sentences which are easy to understand.

● Write a letter to your teacher or head teacher of your primary school, describing a special memory from your primary schooldays. Try to include some interesting descriptive detail and imagery to make the event come alive for the teacher.

● Write an explanation for new Year 7 pupils of how to be safe when working in the science laboratories at secondary school. Think carefully about the points you wish to emphasise, and how to do this most effectively. Remember, also, to consider layout carefully. What features would help your reader to keep safe?

● Think of your favourite activity, sport or club at school. Design a poster that informs new Year 7 pupils what happens during that activity. Your intention is not necessarily to persuade them to join you, but to give them information about what is available for them to do in school.

Unit Three

Writing to persuade, argue, advise

In this unit, you will:

- **think about what is special about writing to persuade, argue, advise**

- **review your own writing, to see what needs to be done to make it a sound Level 4⁺**

- **look at how professional authors write adverts to persuade, argue in letters to newspapers, and give advice on what to do**

- **draft your own writing in these forms.**

Main National Framework Objectives Covered: 7Sn1, 7Sn8, 7Sn13d/e/f, 7Sn15, 7Wr1, 7Wr15, 8Sn1, 8Sn6, 8Sn10, 8Wr2, 8Wr14, 9Wr14

Writing to persuade, argue, advise – what is it?

This kind of writing is very common both in and outside school. If we look at each aspect separately, we can see that:

- Writing to **persuade** should make readers see things from the writer's point of view. It uses emotive language to work on the reader's feelings. It repeats words (repetition) and asks rhetorical questions to make the writer's point strongly. It gives detailed examples to help readers understand what the writer means.
- Writing to **argue** should persuade a reader with a logical argument. It persuades by giving reasons and detailed explanations. It also persuades by discussing opposite viewpoints. It then shows where they are wrong.
- Writing to **advise** should make the reader want to follow the instructions given. It often persuades the reader by sounding friendly. However, if the writing sounds formal, it can persuade because it seems important.

Discuss the following text-types. Which ones are meant to persuade? Which ones are meant to argue or to advise? Sometimes, they may do more than one of these things. Discuss the list and see what you think.

a science fiction novel
a private diary
a newspaper report on a volcanic explosion
a newspaper editorial
a novel set in the Middle Ages
an instruction manual for a video
a recipe for lasagne
an advertisement for a supermarket
an essay about 'Macbeth'
a cricketer's autobiography
a leaflet from Friends of the Earth
a letter from a friend who has moved away
a war story
an essay in history about the causes of the First World War
a letter to your local council, complaining about the lack of safe routes for cyclists
a letter to a newspaper about vandalism
a report on an experiment in science
your favourite joke

What makes a good piece of writing to persuade, argue, advise?

You now have an idea about what writing to persuade, argue and advise is like. For homework, collect as many examples of these types of writing as you can. Look in newspapers and magazines. Look at recipes and instruction manuals. Collect leaflets from shops, local council offices, or tourist offices. Look through the writing you do at school. Look at writing in other subjects, as well as in English.

 Working in groups, look at the examples you have collected. Remember what you know about non-fiction text-types. What **features** of writing to persuade, argue and advise can you pick out? Do you think that some of your examples get their ideas across more clearly or more strongly than others? Can you explain why?

Look for:

- how the writer catches the reader's attention at the start
- the viewpoint chosen by the writer. Is it first person (*I / we*) or third person (*he / she / it / they*)?
- how the writer addresses (speaks to) the reader
- how informal (more like speech) or formal (more like writing) the voice of the writer sounds
- the persuasive techniques used by the writer. Look for emotive language, repetition, or rhetorical questions
- the main tense used by the writer
- any use of modal verbs
- different sentence lengths
- the range of connectives which the writer uses
- when the writer starts new paragraphs
- how the writer develops the topic sentence of paragraphs. Look for extra detail or examples.

As a class, make up a list of the features that you would expect to find in writing to persuade, argue and advise. Don't worry at this stage about how the features affect meaning. Just collect a list of features. You will see how these features are used, later in the unit.

 Record the list in your notebook. You might present what you have learnt as a wall display.

How can you improve your own writing?

Collect two or three pieces of your own writing to persuade, argue and advise. Talk to your partner. How many of the features do you use already? What features do you need to improve?

On this and the following page, there are grids which show in detail the things you need to do for a sound Level 4+. There are a lot of things to think about, but don't worry. A lot of them you will already be doing well. Some, though, you will need to improve on. The grids will help you think about what to improve. If you are not sure about a feature, your teacher will be able to explain. You could also wait to see how the feature is used later in the unit.

Copy the grids into your notebook. (It may also be possible for your teacher to photocopy them.) For each feature, put a tick in the box which applies to you. When you have finished, you will be able to see what you need to focus on in the rest of this unit. You will then be able to track your targets and improvements as you write.

FEATURES OF WRITING	I can do this sometimes	I can usually do this	I need to improve this
I capture the reader's interest with a heading or opening sentence.			
I know how to choose a personal (*I/we*) or impersonal (*he/she/it/they*) viewpoint.			
I make sure that it's clear what pronouns refer back to.			
I know how to speak to the reader in a formal or informal way.			
I have a clear idea of who the reader is, and how I want them to react.			
I choose formal or informal words where I need to.			
I use emotive language to persuade the reader.			
I use repetition to persuade the reader.			
I use rhetorical questions to persuade the reader.			
I know when verbs are in the past, present or future tense.			
I don't vary verb tenses unless there is a good reason.			

FEATURES OF WRITING	I can do this sometimes	I can usually do this	I need to improve this
I use modal verbs.			
I end sentences with a full stop.			
I start sentences with a capital letter.			
I write names with a capital letter.			
I write short sentences for emphasis.			
I know how to pick out subordinate clauses.			
I choose when to separate subordinate clauses from main clauses with commas.			
I use a range of connectives to begin subordinate clauses.			
I use a range of connectives to link sentences and paragraphs.			
I use logical connectives to structure an argument.			
I start a new paragraph to show a change in topic.			
I start a new paragraph to show a change in time.			
I use a topic sentence for each paragraph.			
I develop the topic sentence by explaining in detail or by giving examples.			
I keep a list of the spellings and spelling patterns that I have trouble with.			
I check my drafts carefully for the spellings and patterns I have trouble with.			

 Now that you have reviewed your writing, record in your notebook the main things that you need to work on and improve. Keep checking your progress throughout the unit.

Writing to persuade: advertisements

Adverts are a type of writing to **persuade** which you come across all the time. For example, you find adverts in newspapers and magazines. You also find adverts on billboards in the street, or on buses and trains. We can't get away from them. To see how adverts use language, look at the following example:

How do they do it?

- **Catching the reader's attention.** The writers catch our attention with the layout of the advert. Look at the way they use capital letters and bold print. How do the capitals make the 'voice' of the writers sound? They also use a pun (*free/three*) as a joke. How does that affect the reader?
- **Using repetition.** The word *free* is repeated four times in the first five lines. This persuades the reader because it seems as if it won't cost anything to try the product.
- **Giving examples.** The writers give three examples of how this service is free. Why would each reason be persuasive to the reader?
- **Knowing their reader.** What can you work out about the kind of reader which the writers want to attract? What clues did you use?

- **The text of the advert.** This is all one paragraph. Look at how it works.
  - It mainly uses the **present tense**. However, it also uses the past tense and the future time. How many examples of each tense can you find? Why is each one used?
  - It is **personal**. The writers use the pronouns *we* and *us* to refer to themselves. This makes it seem as if the reader is listening to a team of real people. It makes the 'voice' in the advert sound friendly.
  - It is **informal**. Talking sounds less formal than writing, and this also gives the advert a friendly feeling. The questions make it seem as if the reader is having a conversation. The writers also break long sentences up by starting many of them with *or*. This is what we often do in speech, but not usually in writing. Finally, the writers make their writing sound like speech by missing out letters and words, which we would normally put in when we write. What examples can you find?
  - It starts with a **topic sentence**. This tells you what the paragraph will be about. What is the key word in this topic sentence?
  - The text expands the topic sentence by giving **examples**. How many examples does it give? Which ones are the most persuasive?
  - The text uses **connectives** to link sentences. *That* is a connective which begins a subordinate clause. It gives the reader more information. How many times is it used in this paragraph? The text also makes use of the connectives *and/or*. What different job does each of these two connectives do?
  - The text organises the sentences in the paragraph, building up to the most important reason. It signals the **build-up** to the reader with the connectives *even* and *still*. Can you explain what each of these connectives means? Would the advert be more or less persuasive, if these connectives were missing?

It's your turn

You are going to draft an advert, using the techniques above. Write for new pupils who might come to your school. Persuade them to choose your school, not a neighbouring one. Set it out like the AOL advert on page 50.

First of all, collect ideas. On your own, write a 'brainstorm' list of things which you like about your school. Just keep writing for two or three minutes without stopping. Write down anything that comes into your mind. Don't worry if some ideas sound strange. The point is to get as many ideas to choose from as possible. Then, compare your list with someone else's. From your lists, pick seven or eight ideas which you think would be most persuasive.

Now talk to your partner. Decide on the best order to present your ideas. Which are the first three reasons to choose your school? Which is the best or most important reason, that you want to save until last?

When you start to write your advert, make sure that you:

- Attract your readers' attention with the heading. You could use the AOL idea of *Three reasons to try . . .*, or you could use your own ideas. Whatever you choose, keep it short and snappy.
- When you set out the first three reasons to choose your school, you could repeat a word in each one, like in the AOL advert. You could also use a mixture of capitals and bold print. This would help attract attention. Set the reasons out like in the AOL advert.
- Use mainly present tense, but try some past-tense and future-time verbs. These tenses will help you talk about what life was like at previous schools, and what it will be like at your school.
- Speak to the reader in a friendly, informal way. Use the pronouns *we* and *you*.
- Remember to give detailed examples to back up your reasons. This will make them more persuasive.
- Organise the reasons in your paragraph, so that they build up to the most important point. The AOL advert uses punctuation and sentence-type to show the most important reason. The first four reasons in the paragraph are written as questions. The final one is a statement, not a question. This makes the reader notice it, as the most important reason. You could try this technique yourself.
- Use a range of connectives. Try at least one each of *and/but/or*. Choose at least three of: *first, second, next, also, as well, finally*. They will help you organise your ideas.

Think back to your targets. **Review** your learning in your notebook.

Writing to argue: letters to newspapers

Like the writers of adverts, people who write letters to newspapers want to persuade the reader. In the case of letters, the writers want to make the reader think about what they say, and take it seriously. They therefore argue their point to make it convincing. Look at these two letters. They are about different subjects, but they both use similar techniques.

Mirror M@ilbox

Edited by GERRIE ESAU

HAVE YOUR SAY: Write to Gerrie, Letters Editor, The Mirror, One Canada Square, London E14 5AP   email: deargerrie@mgn.co.uk   *Letters must include full address.*

Let's go full throttle to catch road hogs

THERE has been a lot of criticism about speed cameras recently, but I'm all for the police spending money to clamp down on dangerous drivers.

I recently drove home to Edinburgh from a holiday in Norfolk and I was appalled by the standard of driving on our roads.

I had idiots sitting on my tail refusing to budge, boy racers showing off and lorry drivers thundering past just inches away from my car.

And last, but by no means least, were short-sighted OAP drivers. After they reach a certain age, people should be made to re-sit their tests.

As far as I'm concerned, the sooner we tackle these road hogs the better.

Billy Braidwood, Edinburgh

The Newspaper

Your *shout*

Why are we served last?

I would like to bring people's attention to the problem of child discrimination.

My friends and I have been in many cafes and have waited 15 to 20 minutes to be served. Even then, most times we have been served after adults who have come in after us. There are times when we have waited so long that we ended up walking out.

These incidents really annoy me and I feel that more should be done to solve the problem. After all, our money is just as good as any else's.

Laura (aged 15)

How do they do it?

● **Catching the reader's attention.** The letters page editors catch our attention by choosing a headline (in bold print) to sum up the main idea of the letter. One of them plays with language, to help catch the reader's attention. What does *full throttle* mean? How does it fit with the letter that follows?

● **Addressing the editor.** Although the writers want to persuade the readers of the newspaper, the letters are actually addressed to the editor. Letters to *The Mirror* would begin *Dear Gerrie*, but this salutation is left out when the letter is printed. Where does the editor say that she wants to be addressed like this? How do you think you would address the editor of *The Newspaper*? Which address is more formal? What other information should the writer give?

● **Making it personal.** Because the writers are giving their own opinion, they use the first-person pronoun *I*. The groups of people they are writing about are referred to in the third person, usually as *they*. The writers also use the pronoun *we*. Why do they do that, and what is the effect?

● **Choosing formal or informal language.** Using *I* tends to make writing informal, because it sounds like a person speaking and giving their opinion. You can also make a text sound informal by the kinds of words you choose, and by using abbreviations or contractions like *won't, can't*. Which of these two letters sounds more formal? How did you decide?

● **Structuring the letters.** When you argue, you need to structure what you say in a logical way. Both these letters follow a similar pattern:
  ▪ The first paragraph **introduces** the subject that the writers want to tell you about. Notice how they use the present tense, because they are making a general statement about how things are.
  ▪ The middle paragraphs **give the evidence** for what the writers say in the first paragraph. The evidence makes the argument stronger. It helps persuade the reader to agree with the writers. Notice the way the writers use the past tense to give examples of what happened to them.
  ▪ Notice the sentence structures which **give examples**. The first writer uses a list of -ing verbs to add extra details (*idiots sitting . . . refusing to budge, boy racers showing off, . . . lorry drivers thundering past*). The second writer uses subordinate clauses to give extra detail. (*adults, who have . . ., times when . . .*) Again, these extra details make the argument stronger. They help persuade the reader.
  ▪ The last paragraph gives the writers' **opinions about what should be done**. Notice the way the writers use phrases to signal their **conclusions** (*As far as I'm concerned, After all*). What other connective phrases could they have used to signal their conclusions? Can you find other connective phrases from earlier in their letters? These phrases help structure the information into a logical argument.
  ▪ Notice, also, how both writers use modal verbs (*should, would*). They tell the reader what the writers think ought to happen. In what paragraphs do these modals mainly come? Why are they used in those places?

It's your turn

Draft a letter to a newspaper, using the techniques on page 55. You may have some ideas on what subject to choose. If not, try some of the suggestions at the end of this unit. **Think back** to your targets and, after writing your letter, **review** what you have learnt.

It may not be easy at first to think of ideas. You could try some of the following techniques to help you:

- Talk to friends and partners about things that are important to you, or that you feel strongly about. Talking often helps you find ideas for writing.
- Try to find detailed examples of the things you talk about. The best examples are probably things that have happened to you, or to someone you know.
- Write a list of ideas that come into your mind. Don't stop while you are writing. Just keep your pen moving. Try to list ten or fifteen ideas, as they come into your head. You can then pick the best to write about.
- Develop the idea you have picked, by writing for six or seven minutes without stopping. Begin with *What I want to tell people about is ....* When you finish, look back over what you have written. Are there any new ideas in there which you are pleased with? Are there any which will be useful? Underline them, so that they stand out.

Now organise your ideas into a draft.

- Think about how to address the editor. (Include your address in the top right-hand corner. Also include a heading to sum up your letter. You might like to leave this heading until you have written your draft. It's often easier to think of a title or heading, when you see what you have written.)

- Write from the *I* viewpoint. You could also use the pronouns *we* and *they*. What effect would that have?

- Think also about how formal your letter will be. Will you use abbreviations and contractions like *can't* or *won't*? Or will you make your letter sound more formal by writing *can not* or *would not*?

- In the first paragraph, introduce your subject. Remember to use the present tense, because you are making a general statement.

- Use the middle paragraphs to give the evidence for what you have said in the first paragraph. Remember that the past tense is used to give examples of what has happened to you or to other people.

- Remember the types of sentence structures which give examples to back up your argument. You could use a list of -ing verbs to add extra details. You could use subordinate clauses to give extra detail.

- Remember also connective words and phrases like *first, second, also*, and *as well as*. They will help to structure your argument in a clear and persuasive way.

- Use the last paragraph to give your opinions about what should be done. Remember connective phrases to signal your conclusions in a logical, structured way (*As far as I'm concerned, After all*). Try to use modal verbs (*should, would*) in this paragraph.

Writing to advise: newspapers and magazines

This type of writing is similar to information or instruction writing, rather than to the persuasive and argument writing which you have been studying. You will find many kinds of advice columns in newspapers and magazines, about many kinds of subjects. For example, you could find columns giving advice about money, about computers, about health, or about fitness training. Can you find any more subjects in magazines or newspapers? Here is some advice from a teenage magazine aimed at girls:

I Can't Talk To
BOYS!
Don't panic about chatting to boys. It's easy!

The problem: You're really shy.

Don't say: Nothing!

Do: Concentrate on just being mates with boys before you start thinking about chatting them up. Hang out with them, chatting about school and other stuff, like their hobbies, fave groups etc. Get to know them, without trying to charm them the whole time. You might find it easier to do this with just one lad, rather than with a group of lads, where you could feel you've always got an audience listening to what you're saying, or even laughing at you. Remember, though, that it's OK to be shy with boys if that's how you are, so you don't have to turn into Mad Personality Girl the minute a lad approaches. After all, lots of them are really shy, and don't know how to talk to girls, either.

How do they do it?

- **Catching the reader's attention.** The writer catches our attention with the heading. Why would it be appealing? How do the capital letters and the exclamation mark make the 'voice' of the speaker sound? Why would that help to attract the reader's attention?

- **Speaking to the reader.** The writer uses the pronoun *you*. This makes the advice sound as if it is aimed at an individual. It gives a friendly effect. The writer doesn't refer to himself or herself, though. This gives the advice authority. The command verbs also give the writer authority. How many of them can you find?

- **Using informal language.** The friendly feeling is carried on by the informal words chosen, like *mates*, *lads*, and *stuff*. Some of the verbs are also informal, like *hang out*, *you've*, *it's*. What other examples of informal language can you find? What would the formal version of these words be?

- **Giving alternatives.** The modal verbs *might* and *could* tell the reader that the writer's ideas are only suggestions. The connectives *though* and *rather than* also tell the reader that there are other possibilities. How might this make the reader feel?

- **Organising the advice.** The advice is all given in one paragraph:
  - The paragraph begins with a **topic sentence**, telling you what the paragraph will be about. Can you pick out some key words or phrases from this paragraph?
  - The next two sentences **expand** the topic sentence. They give **examples**. Notice how the sentences start with a command verb, then give more **detail** about what to do, or what not to do.
  - The fourth sentence gives the reader some **alternatives**. The connectives *if* and *so* begin subordinate clauses in this sentence. What does each connective tell you about the information which follows?
  - The final sentence is important, because it makes the most powerful point. It **sums up** what has been said. How would this piece of advice make the reader feel? What is the connective that tells you that the sentence will be important?

It's your turn

Draft a piece of advice for boys, telling them how to talk to girls they are meeting for the first time. Use the same layout as the one you've been previously studying. When you draft the *Do:* section, write one paragraph of about 130 words.
Think back to your targets before beginning your draft. **Review** your learning when you've finished.

- First of all, talk about the advice you've just read in the magazine. Do you agree with it? Would you change it in any way?
- Before you begin your own draft, jot down some ideas in your notebook to get you thinking. You could use a sentence beginning like *I think boys should* .... If you can use some *because* clauses, to explain reasons, it would be helpful.
- When you've finished, you could divide into girls' groups and boys' groups to compare ideas. Each group should decide on the three pieces of advice which they think are best. Remember to have an example for each piece of advice.
- Then compare the girls' ideas with the boys' ideas. How similar are they? Do the boys need any advice from the experts?

When you have got your ideas together, draft your paragraph. You could use this structure:

Sentence 1: Topic sentence. Start with a command verb. What are your key words or phrases? Underline them.

Sentence 2 and Sentence 3: Give examples of what you said in the topic sentence. The following chart shows how the magazine writers give examples. You could try to do it in the same way. Remember to separate parts of sentences with commas.

Command	Example	Example
Hang out with them,	*chatting about school and other stuff,*	*like their hobbies, fave groups, etc.*
(Use a command verb.)	(Give an example, starting with an -ing verb.)	(Add another example, starting with *like*.)
Get to know them	*without trying to charm them the whole time.*	
(Use a command verb.)	(Give an example, using *without*, of what not to do.)	

Sentence 4: Suggest alternatives. Use modal verbs like *might* or *could*.

Sentence 5: Start it with *Remember, though, ...* Don't forget the pair of commas round *though*. Why are they there?

Sentence 6: This sums up your advice, or makes your most important point. Start with one of these connectives: *Finally, . . .; Above all, . . .; After all, ...* Remember the comma!

Revising your drafts

When you've finished a draft, you need to work with a partner to revise them before you write a final version. Check over the following features:

- Is it **clear** what you have said? Ask your partner to read your draft. Ask them to mark places where they aren't sure what you mean. Ask them to mark places where the sentences don't follow on clearly.
- Have you used the right **verb tenses**? (Mainly present tense. If you use present or future time, make sure you know why.)
- Have you a range of **viewpoints** (first-person or third-person pronouns)?
- Are your **pronouns** clear? (Ask your partner to read your draft, highlighting each pronoun. If they aren't sure what the pronoun refers back to, they should put a question mark in the margin. You will then need to make it clear.)

And:

- Have you ended each sentence with a **full stop**? (Count the number of sentences you have written in each paragraph. Write the number in the margin. Then count the number of full stops. The numbers should be the same!)
- Do all your sentences **begin with a capital letter**? (Underline the first word of each sentence. Has it got a capital letter?)
- Have you used **capital letters for names**? (Underline each name in your story. Put a ring round the first letter. Is it a capital?)
- Have you separated some of your **subordinate clauses** from main clauses with **commas**? (Look at the start of each clause to see if it begins with a connective. If there is a connective, put a box around it. Do you need to use a comma?)
- Have you used a **range of connectives**? (Look at the connectives you have marked. Don't overuse *and* or *but*. Have you used most of the connectives you have learnt in this unit? List them and check.)

And:

- Have you used a **topic sentence** when you start a new paragraph? (Underline the topic sentence in each paragraph.)
- Have you **developed** the topic sentence in the rest of the paragraph? (Mark the following sentences with *Explain* or *Example*. This will help you see how each sentence develops the topic sentence.)

And finally:

- Check your draft carefully for the **spelling patterns** you know you have trouble with. (Use your spelling list to remind you.)

When you are ready, review your progress using the grids from pages 48 and 49. What features of writing have you improved? The more improvements you have made, the closer you are to a sound Level 4+.

And you could try . . .

- **Experimenting with formality and informality.** Remember that the more like speech a text sounds, the less formal it is. Work with a partner and list the things which tell you whether writing is formal or informal. Now draw a line in your notebook, and number it from 1 (completely informal) to 10 (completely formal):

  1   5   10

Think about each of the texts you have studied in this unit. Where would you put each one of them on this line? Why? Write the title of each text into that position.

- Look back at the texts in this unit. (You could also look through other newspapers and magazines.) Find examples of sentences which have subordinate clauses in them. In your notebook, make a list of the connectives which begin subordinate clauses. This will help you to build up a wide range of connectives which you could use. Make sure that you know what each connective means, though.
- Look through a range of texts from newspapers and magazine to find examples of adverts, letters and advice columns. Can you find places where writers look at viewpoints that are the opposite of their own? Are there any connective words and phrases that they use, when they are looking at opposing viewpoints? Could you make a list of these connectives?
- When you think about writing a letter to a newspaper, you might write about a topic which your teacher suggests. You might already feel strongly about a topic, which is fine. You might also want to find a topic in a newspaper, which you want to write about. You could choose a local newspaper, a national newspaper like *The Mirror, The Sun* or the *Daily Express*, or a publication aimed at young people, like *The Newspaper*. Look at the letters page. What subjects are the letters about? When you have found a topic to give your opinion about, follow the advice the paper gives on letters to the editor. Remember that the more detail you give in your examples and illustrations, the more persuasive your argument will be. You should normally aim to write about 150 words.
- Apart from advice pages in newspapers, you'll find advice pages in magazines which deal, for example, with sport or computers. How is the advice in these magazines similar to or different from the advice page you have seen on page 57 of this unit? If you or your friends are experts in a particular area, try writing some questions and answers advising on that subject.
- And finally, here's a challenge! Write an advert persuading your audience that school dinners or homework are so brilliant that nobody with any sense would miss out on them. Make the text of your advert, overall, about 90 to 100 words.

Unit Four

Writing to analyse, review, comment

In this unit, you will:

- think about what is special about writing to analyse, review, comment

- review your own writing, to see what needs to be done to make it a sound Level 4⁺

- look at how professional authors write to analyse, review, comment on a book, a film, a restaurant, an important issue or a subject of general interest

- draft your own writing in these forms.

Main National Framework Objectives Covered: 7Sn1a/b/c, 7Sn3, 7Wr18, 7Wr19

Writing to analyse, review, comment – what is it?

When you write to **analyse**, **review** and **comment**, you might be writing about a very wide range of things. The thing you are writing about is called the **subject matter**. The subject matter might be:

- a new book, film or video; a restaurant, song or television programme
- a sports event, like the England football team's progress in the World Cup; an historical event, like the Battle of Hastings; a scientific discovery, like a new drug to fight against cancer; or a human achievement, like the first ascent of a difficult mountain
- an issue, like whether school uniform is a good thing; a speech by a politician on a subject of great national importance, like whether Britain should join the euro.

Whatever the subject matter is, this kind of writing has three main features.

- The writing **reviews** its subject matter. This means the writing describes or explains the subject so that the reader understands it. If it is a new book, the writing will explain briefly what the story is; if it is an historical event, the writing will explain what happened. If it is an issue it will explain what the issue is about.
- The writing will **analyse** the subject matter. This means picking out what is good or bad about it. If it is a book, the writing will say what was interesting and different about the book. It will say what was boring or predictable about it. If it is an event, it will say why something was important or significant about it. If it is an issue where people have very different views, it will say what are the advantages and disadvantages of each viewpoint.
- The writing will **comment** on the subject matter. This means that it will give the writer's own opinions about the book, event, or issue, backed up with evidence.

When writing to **analyse**, **review** and **comment**, the writer always has to remember what the reader wants to know. Its **purpose** is not just to give the writer's own opinions, but also to help the reader make up his or her mind about whether to watch a new film, buy a new book, or vote to join the euro. The writing could be composed in quite a formal style, but it has to be in such a way that will make the reader want to read it. Sometimes this means it might use slang or a chatty style.

Discuss the following text-types. Which ones are meant to analyse, review and comment? Discuss the list and see what you think.

a science fiction novel

a private diary

a scientific report on a new drug to fight flu

a newspaper comment on the Government's plans for the Railways

a novel set in the Middle Ages

an instruction manual for a video

a recipe for lasagne

a magazine article about three new cookery books

an advertisement for a supermarket

a report on two supermarkets' own brand chocolate bars

an essay about the Harry Potter books

a cricketer's autobiography

a leaflet from Friends of the Earth on the effects of building new nuclear power stations

a letter from a friend who has moved away

a speech by a politician on the how schools can be made better

an essay in history about the Battle of Hastings

a letter to your local council, complaining about the lack of safe routes for cyclists

a letter to a newspaper about vandalism

a report on an experiment in science

your favourite joke

a page in a teenage magazine about new films and videos

What makes a good piece of writing to analyse, review, comment?

You now have an idea about what writing to analyse, review and comment is like. For homework, collect as many examples of these types of writing as you can. Look in newspapers and magazines. Look at text books. Look on the Internet. Look through the writing you do at school. Look at writing in other subjects, as well as in English.

Working in groups, look at the examples you have collected. Draw on your knowledge of non-fiction text-types. What **features** of writing to analyse, review and comment can you pick out? Do you think that some of your examples are better than others at getting their ideas across to their audience? Can you explain why?

Look for:

- how the writer catches the reader's attention at the start
- whether the writer addresses the reader with the second-person pronoun *you*
- how informal (more like speech) or formal (more like writing) the voice of the writer sounds
- how clearly the writer explains or describes the subject of his or her writing
- how many examples or quotations the writer uses
- how the writer picks out the good and bad points, or strengths and weaknesses in what he or she is writing about
- how the writer gives his or her own opinion on the subject matter
- the main tense the writer uses and why he or she used that tense
- the use of subordinate clauses
- the range of connectives which the writer uses
- when the writer starts new paragraphs.

As a class, make up a list of the features that you would expect to find in writing to analyse, review and comment. Record the list in your notebook. You might also present what you have learnt as a wall display.

How can you improve your own writing?

Collect two or three pieces of your own writing to analyse, review and comment. Talk to your partner about the features you have been discussing. Some things you will be doing already. What things do you need to improve?

On this and the following page, are grids which show in detail the things you need to do for a sound Level 4[+]. There are a lot of things to think about, but don't worry. A lot of them you will already be good at, but some you will need to improve. The grids will help you think about them. If you are not sure about a feature, your teacher will be able to explain. You could also wait to see how the feature is used during the unit.

Copy the grids into your notebook. (It may also be possible for your teacher to photocopy them.) For each feature, put a tick in the box which applies to you. When you have finished, you will be able to see what you need to focus on in the rest of this unit. You will then be able to track your targets and improvements as you write.

FEATURES OF WRITING	I can do this sometimes	I can usually do this	I need to improve this
I capture the reader's interest with a heading or opening sentence.			
I use the second-person pronoun to speak to the reader.			
I explain something clearly so that a reader will understand what I am talking about.			
I choose to use a formal or informal style to suit the reader of my piece of writing.			
I draw out the good and bad points of my subject matter.			
I use examples and quotations to back up my ideas.			
I choose vocabulary to make my writing more interesting.			
I explain my own opinions clearly and in detail.			
I use the correct verb tense.			

FEATURES OF WRITING	I can do this sometimes	I can usually do this	I need to improve this
I end sentences with a full stop.			
I start sentences with a capital letter.			
I write names with a capital letter.			
I can use subordinate clauses to make my sentences more complex.			
I can use commas to separate subordinate clauses from main clauses.			
I use a range of connectives to begin subordinate clauses.			
I use a range of connectives to link sentences and paragraphs.			
I write in paragraphs.			
I start each paragraph with a topic sentence.			
I develop the topic sentence by explaining in detail or by giving examples.			
I keep a list of the spellings and spelling patterns that I have trouble with.			
I check my drafts carefully for the spellings and patterns I have trouble with.			

Now that you have reviewed your writing, record in your notebook the main things that you need to work on and improve. Keep checking your progress throughout the unit.

Writing to analyse, review, comment: a restaurant review

You can write a review of anything that you have experienced that other people might want to know about. Often in newspapers and magazines, you will find reviews of books and films. Sometimes, you will also find restaurant reviews, which let people know about a restaurant that they might like to visit. In this section, you are going to look at an example of a restaurant review and then write a review of your own.

The key skills you are going to be developing are:

- working out how to decide what is good or bad, effective or successful about your subject matter
- putting your ideas across in a fair, balanced way
- giving your own opinions.

Looking at a restaurant review

BROOK'S RESTAURANT
6/8 Bradford Road, Brighouse

The emphasis is definitely on comfort and relaxation at Brook's. Candle-lit tables, polished floorboards and elegant seating combine to create a soothing atmosphere that is complimented by owner Darrell Brook's passion for jazz – Ella Fitzgerald, Billie Holiday and Fats Waller are always on the menu.

Have a drink in the bar area before your meal and afterwards you can repair to one of the lounges for a coffee and brandy.

"Most people like to relax after a good meal and it means that people don't feel rushed from the table," says Brook. This chilled-out atmosphere does not equate to a lack of care and attention, however. "We aim to be informal but, at the same time, provide a professional and unobtrusive service," he adds.

Both Brooks and executive chef director Richard Ullah were trained as chefs in five-star London hotels.

"Our food is modern British," says Brook. "And I suppose it's quite eclectic." Indeed, there are few restaurants that offer starters of smoked ostrich alongside warm Spam fritters with (homemade) tomato ketchup. Brook says they introduced Spam onto the menu "just for a laugh", little realising it would lead to their being given the Spam Award as "Britain's top place to enjoy a slice of Spam".

If ostrich or Spam is not to your taste then there is plenty to tempt you on the rest of the menu. Starters like Moneybags filled with mushrooms and Brie with a garlic cream sauce and main courses like confit of lamb, roasted garlic, Rosemary and walnut oil jus'.

Or, for vegetarians, spinach and Ricotta ravioli with Chantrelle mushroom cream sauce.

Desserts range from bread and butter pudding to the delectable dark and white chocolate torte with malted sorbet.

With excellent food and friendly but discreet service you're sure to be feeling *Fine and Mellow* afterwards.

DIANE BROUGHTON

How they do it

Read the review of Brook's Restaurant on the previous page and notice these features of the review:

- The first sentence grabs the reader's attention: *The emphasis is definitely on comfort and relaxation at Brook's*. The first thing the reader will notice is that this restaurant is a pleasant and relaxing place to be.
- There is detailed description of the restaurant: *Candle-lit tables, polished floorboards and elegant seating combine to create a soothing atmosphere . . . .* This helps the reader picture the place in their mind.
- There are quotations from the owner to illustrate the good features of the restaurant: *'We aim to be informal but, at the same time . . .' he adds*. These give the reader a wider range of opinions. They do not only have the writer's view, but the view of other people too.
- There are complex sentences with several subordinate clauses: *Have a drink in the bar area before your meal and afterwards you can repair to one of the lounges for a coffee and brandy*. The extra information added by the subordinate clause: *and afterwards* gives the reader more detail about the restaurant: it has a lounge where you can relax after your meal. Using a long sentence also helps the review sound quite formal, which fits since the restaurant sounds like quite an upmarket one. Lastly, the long sentence helps create a calm effect, which fits with the relaxing atmosphere the writer experienced in the restaurant.
- The choice of adjectives shows the writer's opinions. Notice the adjectives in this sentence: *With excellent food and friendly service . . . .*
- There is detailed information on the most important point: the food.
- The second-person pronoun *you* is used to talk directly to the reader: *If ostrich or Spam is not to **your** taste then there is plenty to tempt **you** on the rest of the menu*.
- The present tense is used throughout.

Look again at the review on page 71 and then discuss these questions with a partner.

- What is the main **purpose** of the review?
- What **audience** is the review aimed at? What clues tell you that?
- What sort of **information** does the review mainly give you?
- Why do you think there is an interview with the owner?
- What does the reviewer think of the restaurant?
- What **adjectives** or **verbs** can you find that help you work out what the writer thinks of the restaurant?
- How can you tell?
- Why is the review written in the present tense?
- Why does it use the second-person pronoun *you*?
- What effect do the **complex sentences** have on how formal or informal the writing sounds?
- How many different **connectives** can you find?
- Are there any paragraphs which do not start with a good **topic sentence**?

It's your turn

You are going to write a review for your school canteen. If you prefer, you could choose to write a review of a different restaurant, one you have been to or like going to, or you could even write a restaurant review of your kitchen at home. If so, don't forget to say nice things about the cook!

Planning your review

Before you can write your review, you will need to decide what will help you work out what the good and bad points of the place are.

To help you work out how to decide what the good and bad points are, look at the list below. Decide which of these are important in deciding how good a restaurant is. Give each a score from 1 to 5, where 1 is not important and 5 is very important.

- quality of food
- wide choice of food
- friendliness of service
- clean room
- price of food
- quiet / loud atmosphere
- nice tables and chairs
- background music
- unusual food
- presentation of food
- quick service.

Now you have worked out what things are important to you in judging a restaurant, you should be clear about how to decide how good your restaurant is.

Gathering information

You need to make notes for your review. You could put them under these four headings:

- description of the restaurant
- description of the food
- other people's opinions about the restaurant
- your opinions about the restaurant.

For each heading note down the good and bad points about the restaurant.

Writing your review

To write a good review at Level 4⁺ you will need to demonstrate your ability to:

- start with a good first sentence
- vary the structure of your sentences
- start with subordinate clauses
- keep the reader's interest
- add descriptive vocabulary
- include quotations from people.

These next activities will help you develop these skills.

- start with a good first sentence

You need to start your review with a good first sentence to grab the reader's attention. Look at these first sentences below and decide which are most likely to make the reader want to carry on reading.

As I walked through the door of The Casa Blanca, I was greeted by the smell of freshly-baked bread and the soft sounds of gentle guitar music.

I am going to write a review of the school canteen.

'Welcome to the best diner in town!' smiled the friendly face on the door of Jo's Diner.

If you want to eat well and cheaply then this kitchen is definitely the place for you.

Yesterday I had the worst meal of my life. Let me tell you about it.

 What do you think makes a good first sentence? Now have a go at writing your first sentence. Do two or three and then decide which you like best. Talk to at least one other person, to see if they agree with you. You can come back and change it later if you want.

- **vary the structure of your sentences**

One of the ways of making your sentences more varied is to use connectives either at the beginning of your sentences, or to join two clauses together.

Look at these examples.

Normally I do not like chicken. Their chicken was really delicious.

You can join these two clauses with a **connective**:

Normally I do not like chicken, <u>but</u> their chicken was really delicious.

Or you could make the two sentences into one by starting the sentence with a connective:

<u>Although</u> normally I do not like chicken, their chicken was really delicious.

Now try some of your own. Practise starting sentences and joining clauses together about your restaurant with these words:

When, while, although, even though, despite, whenever, if, and, but, because, or

Remember you can also use a relative pronoun (*who, which* or *that*) in the same way:

I had the burger, <u>which</u> was the best burger I have ever eaten.

- **add descriptive vocabulary**

You need to add really well-chosen vocabulary to make your writing interesting for the reader. This will also give the reader an idea of what you think of the place. In the next example, which words make the sentence interesting? What impression do the words give of the food served in the restaurant?

The creamy smoothness of the rich chocolate sauce contrasted beautifully with the delicate light 'melt in your mouth' sponge.

Look at the following description. It is badly in need of some improvement. Rewrite it so that the restaurant sounds wonderful. Then rewrite it again so that the restaurant sounds awful! Add adjectives where there is a star, and try to change the words or phrases that have been underlined. Don't forget always to put adjectives before the noun.

We sat on * chairs in the * main room. The * waitress took our order and we <u>looked at</u> the * surroundings as we waited for our meal. The * salad <u>tasted alright</u>, and the * soup <u>was fine</u>. The lasagne for the main course tasted <u>warm</u> and the * ice-cream was <u>chocolate flavour</u>.

● **include quotations from people**

You need to include the opinions of other people in your review as quotations. You can include the opinions of friends who have been there or of people who own the place or work there. When you include a quotation from someone, remember to put speech marks around the person's words. Make sure that the quotation backs up what you have said, or that you explain or add to what they have said.

Look at these two examples below. Which one includes quotation that adds to or explains the point being made and which one uses quotation that is about something different?

The atmosphere in Mrs Smith's café is always friendly and welcoming. She told us, 'I always use food that is as fresh as possible.'

I particularly enjoyed the live music. Tracey, who books the bands that play, told us, 'Having a live band can really add to the atmosphere. It can make your evening a little bit special.'

Drafting your review

You are now ready to write your review. Decide where you want your review to be printed (e.g. in a teenage magazine or in a newspaper). Is it aimed at young people or adults? This will affect the tone and the sort of language you will use.

Look at your plan and remind yourself of all the important information you need to include. Work out a paragraph plan. Remember you need to start a new paragraph whenever you change the topic, change the time or include speech.

Your plan might look like this:

Describing the restaurant from the outside
Describing the inside
Describing ordering, the greeting and the service
Describing the food
Other people's opinions about the place
Your final opinions about the restaurant

Use phrases like:

When I first saw . . .
Once inside, I noticed . . .
I was impressed by . . .
I decided to have . . .
Later, I tried . . .
We spoke to . . . she told us . . .
Overall, I felt . . .

When you are ready to start writing, remember it is very important that you:

- Make it clear to the reader what the restaurant is like, what its good and bad points are. This is where you **review** and **analyse** the restaurant.
- Give your own opinion about the restaurant with reasons or evidence to back it up. This is where you **comment** on the restaurant.
- Use the skills you have been developing:
  - start with a good first line to grab your reader's attention
  - use a range of connectives and relative pronouns to vary the structure of your sentences
  - use well-chosen descriptive vocabulary
  - include quotations from people.

Revising your draft

When you have finished your draft, work with a partner to revise it before you write your final version. Check over the following features:

- Have you explained clearly the **good and bad points** of your subject matter?
- Have you started with an interesting **first sentence**?
- Have you included interesting **descriptive vocabulary**? Underline the adjectives which you think give a good description of what you are writing about.
- Have you included **quotations from people**?
- Have you given your own **opinions**?
- Have you ended each sentence with a **full stop**? (Count the number of sentences you have written in each paragraph. Write the number in the margin. Then count the number of full stops. The numbers should be the same!)
- Do all your sentences **begin with a capital letter**? Have you used **capital letters for names**? (Underline each name in your story. Put a ring round the first letter. Is it a capital?)
- Have you used a **range of connectives** to start and join your sentences?
- Have you separated your **subordinate clauses** from main clauses with **commas**?

And:

- Have you used a **topic sentence** when you start a new paragraph? (Underline the topic sentence in each paragraph.)
- Have you **developed** the topic sentence in the rest of the paragraph? (Mark the following sentences with 'explain' or 'example'. This will help you see how each sentence develops the topic sentence.)

And finally:

- Check your draft carefully for the **spelling patterns** you know you have trouble with. (Use your spelling list to remind you.)

When you are ready, review your progress using the grids from pages 69 and 70. What features of writing have you improved? The more improvements you have made, the closer you are to a sound Level 4$^+$.

 Now write the final version of your review. Make sure that your handwriting and overall presentation are as neat as possible.

And you could try ...

Writing a book review

Choose a book you have read recently on your own or in class.

You will need to explain briefly what the story is about, who the characters are, and where and when it is set. Say how it is similar to other books by that author or in that genre (or type) of story.

To explain your opinions about what was good or bad about the book, you will need to write a separate paragraph about what you liked about the characters and the plot.

Use these questions to help you:

- Did the characters make you want to find out what happened to them?
- Did they make you feel angry or sorry for them?
- How was the plot gripping or believable?
- Did the plot make you want to turn the pages? What was the most exciting part?
- Explain what you liked about the style and the language.
- Was there enough description to help you picture the events of the story?
- Were the chapters about the right length?

Explain what sort of reader would like the book and why.

As with your restaurant review, remember to:

- Start your review with a good first sentence to grab the reader's attention.
- Use well-chosen vocabulary to hold the reader's attention and to show what you thought of the book.
- Use a range of connectives to vary the way you start and join sentences.
- Give detailed examples to back up your opinions. Include quotations from characters. You can also include quotations from other people who have read the book.

You could also write a review of a TV programme, film or video that you have watched.